Placemaking

Improving Small Towns, Neighborhoods, and Downtowns Without Spending a Lot of Money

AL ZELINKA AND SUSAN JACKSON HARDEN

TABLE OF CONTENTS

Foreword iii
Where Did All the Places Go? by Philip Langdon

Preface ix

Acknowledgments xi

Chapter 1. What Is Placemaking on a Budget? 1
The Importance of Placemaking on a Budget 3
Using Placemaking on a Budget 6

Chapter 2. Identifying Meaningful Projects 11
The Two Approaches to Making Placement on a Budget a Reality 12
Community Value-Based Projects 13
Case Study 2.1: The Downtown Enumclaw, Washington,
  Streetscape Enhancement Project 20
Community Canvas-Based Projects 37
Case Study 2.2: The Revival of Confetti Park, New Orleans, Louisiana ... 65
Understanding the Values of Comunity and Place 66
Conclusion 70

Chapter 3. Placemaking on a Budget Resources 73
People 74
Case Study 3.1: Bringing Unity to the Community, Phoenix, Arizona 81
Case Study 3.2: Changing Out at the Volunteer Café, Ocean Beach, California ... 85
Organizations 86
Case Study 3.3: Nappanee Seniors Return to School, Nappanee, Indiana ... 93
Private Sector 94
Case Study 3.4: Realizing the Power of Partnerships in St. Andrews,
  Panama City, Florida 98
Case Study 3.5: Miracle on 4th Street Park, Long Beach, California 99
Policies and Programming 101
Creative Fundraising 105
Case Study 3.6: Returning the Town Common One Brick At a Time,
  Goffstown, New Hampshire 110
Case Study 3.7: Charlie, "The Can Man," Groveland and
  Big Oaks Flat, California 111
Conclusion 112

Chapter 4. Implementation 115
Create Order Out of Chaos 117
Organization Tools for Implementation Effectiveness 117
Conclusion 122

Appendix A. Toolkits 123

Appendix B. List of References 133

Foreword:
Where Did All the Places Go?

By Philip Langdon

hen I was 12 years old, my mother, stepfather, younger brother, and I moved to Wesleyville, a borough of one square mile on the eastern edge of Erie, Pennsylvania. The year was 1959, and Erie was a city that made things, lots of things — Hammermill paper, General Electric locomotives, A.O. Smith pumps, Koldraft ice machines, Bucyrus-Erie construction equipment, Marx toys, and hundreds of other products. Factories, foundries, and tool-and-die shops were Erie's lifeblood. A sprawling complex that GE built beginning in 1910, half a mile from Lake Erie, employed 6,000 workers. If you listened to Erie radio in the first half of the 1960s, you'd hear a savings and loan association commercial in which a male wage earner chirped, in a singsong voice, "I do my work and I get my pay, and I always put some pay away." The refrain captured something fundamental to Erie: an emphasis on regularity, on steady, dependable habits. Families swam and picnicked at Presque Isle beaches every summer, many fathers and sons went deer hunting every fall, and people of all ages reported to their jobs or schools during the long winters no matter how furiously the snow was blowing in from the northwest.

"Sense of place" was a phrase not yet coined. When, in 1958, Mrs. Held, my fifth-grade teacher at Erie's Glenwood Elementary School, had harangued our class about Erie's failure to preserve enough of its past, she was ahead of her time. The city had a few historic sights—most notably, the Mad Anthony Wayne blockhouse and the Brig Niagara, the ship with which Oliver Hazard Perry defeated the British in the Battle of Lake Erie—but like most industrial centers, the Erie area focused more on work and family than on heightening the community's distinctiveness.

On Buffalo Road at Bird Drive, at the Erie–Wesleyville boundary, there was a small black and white sign inviting people to visit Wesleyville's four churches. Except for that sign, motorists might have no idea they were leaving one municipality and entering another. No landmarks or special plantings punctuated the transition. Nonetheless, every Wesleyville resident from grade school on up knew precisely where the 138,000-population city of Erie ended and where our 3,500-person borough began. Awareness was nurtured by local institutions, including the Wesleyville School District and its one school—a red brick structure that stood on Willow Street in the center of the borough, accommodating all of Wesleyville's children from their first day of kindergarten to their last day of high school. Wesleyville had its own government, which employed a police department (sometimes consisting of just one officer) and a small but speedy public works department, which responded to every snowfall by sending out a truck with a man standing on its bed, shoveling a black arc of cinders onto each icy intersection.

The community also had its own shopping district; several blocks of Buffalo Road were lined by one- and two-story buildings containing small stores and eating and drinking establishments. Customers would go to the rambling, wooden Plubell Hardware store, carrying a handful or a bagful of broken pieces and asking for replacements; owner John Schiefferle and his employees would hasten to the hundreds of bins and cabinets throughout the store—containing nuts, bolts, nails, screws, and other items—and furnish exactly what was needed. Schoolchildren congregated at Catrabone's Variety, excitedly discussing shows at the nearby Penn Theatre. (We had no idea that the movie theater, Buffalo Road's biggest attraction, would soon close and be occupied first by people writhing in religious ecstasy—"Holy Rollers," we called them—and later by the Erie Playhouse, which put on stage productions.) Down the block from Ballenger's 5¢ to $1 Store and Jay and Dee's Prescription Drug stood the Wesleyville Bakery, a thriving shop where residents bought bread and rolls, cupcakes and creampuffs. Walking around town wore your shoes out, so people visited the repair shop, where the owner—genial, crewcut Andy Martin—always erred on the side of optimism, promising new heels or soles earlier than he could actually get the job done. When your shoes really were ready, he would hand them over, cheerfully announce the price, and add with a flourish, "and [however many] cents for the governor."

Thinking back on the cities and towns I knew in the fifties and early sixties, I realize that most of them engaged in relatively little "placemaking." Rarely did they adorn their business streets with trees or flowers. Downtown sidewalks were plain concrete. Sculpture appeared at only a few commemorative locations. Sidewalk cafes? Those were for Paris, not for American towns.

This is not to say there weren't communities in which the physical environment had been laid out with great care. Wesleyville's neighbor to the north, Lawrence Park Township, was developed by General Electric, beginning in 1911, as an industrial suburb in the lovely tradition of the English garden city. Lawrence Park had a greenbelt along Four Mile Creek, neatly separating the factory compound—more than 300 acres of flat terrain—from the rest of the town. Named for naval hero James Lawrence, the master-planned town featured an artful arrangement of straight and curvilinear streets interspersed with green spaces of varied character. By contrast, Wesleyville grew up incrementally, without much of an overall plan. The street layout consisted mainly of grids—short, squarish blocks in the oldest parts of town and longer rectangular blocks in the areas where rows of wood or brick bungalows sprouted in the 1920s.

So it wasn't physical design that made Wesleyville distinctive (though the irregular grid of narrow streets did make it easy to get around town and see fellow residents). Mainly it was the network of local institutions and local merchants that made Wesleyville a tight-knit place. It's amazing the number of shopkeepers who were able to survive and raise families on the limited trade of a small community. Tony Bonito supported his family by operating a tiny store, now gone, a few steps from the school; in effect, he had the schoolchildren's candy concession, there being no candy and snack machines in the school. Toby Aaronson supported his wife and sons by operating a shoe store in front of his Buffalo Road home. Distributed around the borough were corner stores, some with residential quarters upstairs. Russ' Dinor (the odd spelling of "diner" was a northwest Pennsylvania idiosyncrasy) advertised in the high school yearbook, "Eat here or we'll both starve." As far as I could tell, nobody starved. People in retail and service businesses made a living—not lavish but in many instances decent enough to send their children to college—by catering to local residents whom they encountered day after day in the shops, on the streets, and at local events.

Today some elements of that way of life persist, but they have been noticeably weakened—in Wesleyville and in most American communities. John Schiefferle leveled his hardware store in 1971 after he couldn't find anyone to purchase the business and keep it in operation. The store, which stocked tools, kitchenware, and sporting goods along with devices needed by farmers and area businesses, couldn't compete with the discounters that opened along the highway in the newer suburban territory to the east. The Penn Theatre bit the dust. Ballenger's closed. The bakery went dark. Although Catrabone's, the dinor, and a number of other establishments persevered, shopping dollars increasingly gravitated to bigger stores outside of town. Let's be frank about this: Wesleyville residents didn't exhibit enough loyalty to keep their local merchants in business. Things were cheaper at shopping centers like Eastway Plaza, which opened just east of Wesleyville in 1959, so people went there and caused the old Buffalo Road shopping district to decline. This did not happen only in Wesleyville; it happened all over the nation. Through billions of individual decisions, one purchase at a time, America threw away its local merchant class—the corps of business owners who served on local committees, bought ads in the high school yearbook, attended local events, and supported innumerable civic causes. Americans were consumers first, citizens of their particular town second (if that).

Granted, the stores that small-scale merchants operated were not all top-quality, and their buildings were rarely the sort to win architectural awards. But they possessed a transcendent virtue: they offered a setting where community life could and did unfold. The buildings on the Wesleyville stretch of Buffalo Road stood close together, many of them forming a continuous series of storefronts. They were no more than 100 or 150 feet away from the beginning of residential neighborhoods, with the result that everyone in the borough had a place to see neighbors, refresh spirits, and find out what was going on in town, all in the course of carrying out the week's errands. In the newer generation of stores, the owner or manager usually didn't know the customers, their families, and their histories. Changes such as these, in the Erie area and throughout the country, have resulted in commercial landscapes that are much less personal, much less intimately connected to the lives of residents.

So it wasn't physical design that made Wesleyville distinctive (though the irregular grid of narrow streets did make it easy to get around town and see fellow residents). Mainly it was the network of local institutions and local merchants that made Wesleyville a tight-knit place.

Yet the need for connection remains as fierce as ever. Most of us long to live or work or spend time in a *place*—a setting that holds meaning for us. From this yearning has sprung a growing expertise in how to make streets, blocks, buildings, and public spaces distinctive and appealing. Today we know more than ever about how to shape the physical environment to satisfy deep human desires. Al Zelinka and Susan Jackson present a wide array of placemaking techniques in this helpful book, techniques that are not necessarily expensive.

Consider local history, one of the tools that people can use to accentuate their community's identity. When I moved away from Wesleyville at the end of the 1960s, I was aware that Wesleyville had been named for the founder of Methodism, John Wesley, but that was pretty much all I knew of the community's history. What I didn't realize was that Wesleyville in the nineteenth century was a hotbed of moral passion. It was a testament to the religious and social ideals shaping the westward-migrating nation. The community apparently received its name because of a Methodist circuit rider who preached near Four Mile Creek, the eastern edge of the village. In the late 1700s and the 1800s, Methodist evangelists on horseback traveled tirelessly from one frontier settlement to another, striving to bring sparsely populated areas into the religious fold. Because of circuit riders, Methodism, a negligible influence in 1780, ranked a century later as Pennsylvania's largest Protestant denomination.

With th e church's growth came fervent social reform efforts. In the mid-nineteenth century, the Wesley Methodist Church, then located on Buffalo Road, became a station on the Underground Railroad. Slaves fleeing the South hid in the church belfry. From the church, they made their way to a stone house that still stands in Lawrence Park. A tunnel led from the stone house toward the Lake Erie shore, embarkation point for a boat trip across 25 miles of unpredictable open water to Canada and freedom. Abolitionist sentiment in Wesleyville must have run strong. Three men from Wesleyville planned to join John Brown for his raid on Harper's Ferry; they apparently missed the event only because Brown launched the attack before they were able to get there.

Religiously inspired zeal briefly made Wesleyville a flashpoint of the prohibitionist movement in the mid-1800s. On Valentine's Day in 1857, Laura McLean, wife of Methodist minister John McLean, led a group that battered the tavern of William McCrum, using clubs, stakes, axes, and other weapons and leaving it a shambles. "A new stock of liquors had just been received and the ladies lost no time in overturning the barrels and knocking the heads out with their weapons," according to one account. "In minutes the 'whiskey and beer on the floor was over the ladies' shoe tops and flowing in streams out the door into the street.'"

If a borough the size of Wesleyville has such interesting stories to tell, surely many other communities also have riveting histories—or landscapes, cultures, industries, or architectural achievements capable of engaging their residents' imaginations. The adept use of resources such as these can help people become more attached to their community, more conscious of its character, more alert to its potential. I see some evidence of that desire during my return visits to Wesleyville. Local people have developed a fine park at Four Mile Creek. They have created a memorial on Buffalo Road. Recently they have been organizing a local museum.

During the past half-century, community ties in most towns and cities eroded, and physical differences between one locale and another diminished. Automobility and economic Darwinism eradicated much of the rooted merchant class that had played such a large part in making a community out of disparate individuals. National franchises and their unwillingness to build retail structures for a long future spawned a commercial strip of impermanent, standardized junk—an environment at odds with community pride and loyalty. Yet a stubborn fact remains: most of us need places that matter to us, especially places in our own city, town, village, or neighborhood. That is why we must master the art and economics of placemaking. It is late in the game—we have already stupidly trashed many of the settings that used to nurture a satisfying community life—but segments of America are waking up. If we devote enough time and skill to making our environments more humanly satisfying, we may yet overcome the long decline of local connectedness. This is truly a worthy mission. It is one of the great challenges of a fickle, throwaway age.

Philip Langdon is senior editor of New Urban News, *a frequent contributor to* Planning *magazine, and author of several books, including* A Better Place to Live: Reshaping the American Suburb *(University of Massachusetts Press, 1994). He lives in New Haven, Connecticut.*

> Yet a stubborn fact remains: most of us need places that matter to us, especially places in our own city, town, village, or neighborhood.

Preface

For more than five decades, the art of making places in our communities special and important to the people who live there has been tossed aside in favor of mass-produced, auto-dominated, formula-style "Anywhere, U.S.A." development. As a country, we have been so focused on growing and building that engaging and involving community members in public and private projects also has been ill considered or deemed unnecessary. As a result, we are now faced with an expanse of communities that are not nurturing us. In many instances, we have exchanged important pieces of our history, culture, and natural resources for cold and lifeless places with no heart or local identity.

Placemaking on a Budget is centered on two very important premises and written as an easy-to-use tool for people interested in adding meaning to their community's public spaces. The first premise is that through the public realm it is possible to enhance community identity and increase connections between people and between people and place. The second premise is that the old adage "time is money" also works in reverse—the time invested in the careful identification of placemaking projects and the active involvement of people will result in money and other resources needed to bring ideas to life.

Our professional revitalization efforts in small towns, downtowns, and neighborhoods across the country, as well as our personal volunteerism experience with Peace Corps, Americorps, and Volunteers in Service to America, have demonstrated to us that people and organizations—when working toward a collective goal—can achieve greatness in even the most disadvantaged environments. We have observed that most people want to feel more connected to each other and to their community; elders often must reflect back 40, 50, or 60 years to recall the strong sense of community and vitality people are seeking today. We have witnessed an individual who believed in his community so much that he independently raised significant funds for a new library and museum by collecting aluminum cans over a 10-year period. We have seen Main Streets with empty sidewalks regain their vitality because of the determination and will of a few concerned merchants and committed public agency staff. We have spent time in neighborhoods where many telltale signs of disinvestment are "overwritten" because a few children's' ideas captivated the attention and spirit of the larger community. From these experiences, we believe that people themselves—regardless of geographical context, built-environment conditions, or financial resources—hold the greatest untapped potential to improve their sense of place and connection to community.

Through our planning practice and community service, we have learned that most communities are faced with the persistent need to do more with less. We have reviewed many other design approaches and techniques for placemaking, as well as case studies on failed, sterile, or poorly designed areas that have been transformed into vital, important parts of communities. Based on this background research, we realized what is missing in planning and design literature and practice is a means of demonstrating how communities of all sizes and types can organize planning efforts and leverage a multitude of resources to develop various public projects that will yield significant, positive change—all the while respecting local authenticity.

To help address this void of information and to make a difference in communities across the country, we have written this publication. It is our intent to provide readers with an easy-to-understand-and-implement resource that provides guidance and inspiration to those who want to make a difference in their home communities. While obstacles to placemaking do exist, none can overcome the collective will of a community. If nothing else, we hope *Placemaking on a Budget* demonstrates this point.

The authors

Acknowledgments

Accomplishments, like this publication, are not solely the result of an individual effort. We have learned that much of what we achieve has roots with people and places that have been and continue to be a part of our lives. While writing *Placemaking on a Budget* took longer than expected, as many works do, the journey to realizing it in print has been enriched by the experiential learning gained from innumerable communities—from Fairbanks, Alaska, and Vienna, Austria, to Milwaukee, Wisconsin, and New Orleans, Louisiana. We are thankful to all the towns and hope that their examples will inspire others to apply *Placemaking on a Budget* principles within their own communities.

Many organizations provided support and encouragement during the writing of *Placemaking on a Budget.* Two require special acknowledgement. First, the American Planning Association, which provided us with the opportunity to speak on the subject in 2001 and then publish our thoughts, beliefs, and ideas in this Planning Advisory Service Report. Jim Hecimovich deserves special thanks, as his patience and belief in our message has been unwavering during the extended writing period.

Second, our appreciation is extended to RBF Consulting for not only its moral support, but also notable financial support. The full-color enjoyed by readers of *Placemaking on a Budget* is due to RBF Consulting's financial sponsorship of the publication. Mike Burke, executive vice president of RBF Consulting and leader of the Planning Department, has been a source of enthusiasm and support for our endeavor—thank you. Other RBF Consulting colleagues have also contributed to this publication and deserve our thanks. To all of RBF Consulting, particularly the talented designers and illustrators Faye Stroud, Jeanette Cappiello, and Bob Klekner, and to our Urban Design Studio Team, we appreciate your support.

We are grateful to many individuals. To Michael Blake Roberts, we do not know where to begin in thanking you for compiling the materials for and writing so many case studies and sidebars. Your efforts have added great value to *Placemaking on a Budget*—value that will benefit many untold people and communities. To George Gehlert, thank you for conceiving of and illustrating the cartoons that begin each chapter. Your talents go far beyond your daily service as a planner—your wit and illustrative abilities, combined with your natural cartooning skills, are gifts to those who have the good fortune of knowing you. For submitting materials for case studies and sidebars, we owe our deepest thanks to the many different authors and resources from around the country noted in the text—they are the important people out there in the trenches strengthening communities one project at a time.

• • •

Thank you Mom, Dad, Lori, and Michael—your never-ending belief in me and in my abilities have helped to shape the person that I am. To my beautiful nieces Rachel and Hannah—it is in part for your future that I want to work so hard to improve the world. And to my soul mate and husband Mike—without your quiet support and love, I don't know where I would be. Thank you also to my professional mentors and friends who have been both teachers and sources of inspiration. To Peter Dreyfuss (I know you have been waiting for this publication for a *long* time!)—thank you for giving me my first opportunity in neighborhood revitalization and for believing in me when I was fresh out of college. To Deb Sydenham, you taught me so much about what meaningful (and fun) community involvement means. To Bruce Race, your personal style and dedication have had such a positive influence on the way that I work with communities. Thank you also to Al Zelinka, we have worked together in many towns and neighborhoods and "making a difference" has been so much fun.

Susan Jackson Harden

● ● ●

Making a difference is hard work, but it is made easier with a core group of family and friends who provide me with a solid foundation and constant inspiration. My contributions to *Placemaking on a Budget* could not have been possible without the support of Anna Pehoushek, my loving wife and life partner. To Mom and Dad, Robin, Marsha, and Marlou, my gratitude goes to you for always believing in me. I would be remiss not to acknowledge the entertaining role of our dogs—Smokey and Ali—during the writing of *Placemaking on a Budget*. Last but not least, I want to thank my coauthor and colleague, Susan Jackson Harden, for her unparalleled dedication to community service and helping communities realize their potential—*Placemaking on a Budget* embodies this commitment.

Al Zelinka

George Gehlert

All too often, well-intended efforts to enhance the qualities of a place are carried out in a manner that sidesteps authentic community attributes in favor of fabricated, transplanted, or out-of-context placemaking schemes, which have a limited shelf life.

CHAPTER 1

What Is Placemaking on a Budget?

he term "placemaking" has a variety of interpretations and meanings—no single, commonly accepted definition exists. To the neighborhood resident or downtown merchant, it may be an odd or foreign word. To the elected or appointed public official, it may sound like another trend in the continuous quest for a better quality of life. To the planner or designer, it can mean something as simple as creating better community spaces. For the purposes of this publication, placemaking means:

> The process of adding value and meaning to the public realm through community-based revitalization projects rooted in local values, history, culture, and natural environment.

WHAT IS A SENSE OF PLACE?

By Michael Blake Roberts

For many people, a particular place can conjure up a multitude of emotions, including nostalgia, belonging, excitement, and possibly fear. We refer to this sentiment as a sense of place, a phrase that hints at the particular ambiance of a space. These feelings inspire recurring battles between those who do and do not seek community change and endow the act of placemaking with considerable power. What is a sense of place, though, and what does the meaning of sense of place suggest about the practice of placemaking?

"Sense of place" draws from the Latin term *genius loci*, which originally referred to the divine protector of a place. Ancient Greeks and Romans believed that resident spirits defined the character of areas, large or small, and celebrated the influence of the local deity through rituals and festivals. As Western culture became more secular, *genius loci* was translated in the eighteenth century as "the genius of a place" in order to describe a space's inspirational qualities (Jackson 1994). The term has shifted over the last three centuries to encompass more sentimental views of space.

Our understanding of sense of place has grown over the last few decades with the beginning of academic study of the topic. Research has often been focused on how a person creates a "place" out of a "space." Scholars have argued that individuals identify with a place in order to shape their own identity, seek a sense of community, and find reassurance in changing times (Brown and Perkins 1992; Cohen 1985; Entrikin 1996; Jackson 1994). Yet there are a number of relevant questions that we still need to ask about the individual: Resident or visitor? Male or female? What does this person use the space for? And so on. Different people construct different senses of the same space.

Many academics, who prefer a sociological rather than psychological approach, contend that social processes are essential to placemaking (Stokowski 2002). Personal characteristics, whether ethnic, racial, sexual orientation, religious, class, or otherwise, shape an individual's perspective. Shared stories, which convey common beliefs, values, and histories, establish a group bond and create a true place (Cresswell 1996; Jacobi and Stokols 1983; Johnstone 1990; Relph 1976; Ryden 1993). As writer Wallace Stegner remarked, "No place is a place until things that have happened in it are remembered in history, ballads, yarns, legends, or monuments. Fictions serve as well as facts" (Stegner 1992).

Since a city or neighborhood consists of many groups, there can be diverse and potentially conflicting images for an area (Lepofsky and Fraser 2003). Place meanings can include some people while excluding others and allow some groups to possess political and economic power over other groups (Bird 2002; Greider and Garkovich 1994; Stokowski 2002; Vandergeest and DuPuis 1996). An example would be a neighborhood that celebrates one ethnic group through festivals and historic preservation and ignores other groups. Therefore, the central tasks of placemaking are "inherently political and moral acts" that should incorporate a high level of collaboration within the entire community (Schneekloth and Shibley 1995). Collaboration can ensure that, together, different groups can arrive at mutually beneficial solutions.

Placemaking has become critical in a time when globalization has weakened the distinctiveness of American cities and regions and left people feeling that they could be anywhere (Kunstler 1993). The benefit for cities and residents is considerable. Policies that foster sense of place, such as historic preservation, a Main Street approach, pedestrian-friendly design, and waterfront development, have been particularly successful in revitalizing small city downtowns (Dane 1997; Robertson 1999). Residents who feel a strong attachment are more likely to know their neighbors, be involved in their community, and feel more secure (Kemmis 1990; Reed, Payton, and Bond 1998; Schneekloth and Shibley 1995; Stedman 2002;). The research on sense of place shows that placemaking should be done with care.

"Placemaking" and "on a Budget" have been combined to not only articulate a process for redefining and rethinking about the places in which we live but also for doing so in a way that is most affordable and realistically attainable by communities with limited resources. *Placemaking on a Budget: Improving Small Towns, Neighborhoods, and Downtowns Without Spending a Lot of Money* is intended to provide planners, designers, and citizens alike with a practical publication that can easily be used to realize placemaking aspirations that make a difference in communities.

THE IMPORTANCE OF PLACEMAKING ON A BUDGET

Unfortunately, in both the physical and social sense, many of our communities are not nurturing us. Routinely, we experience cold and lifeless places in our communities with little to no regard for the people who live in and near these spaces. Asphalt parking lots; strip malls; office parks; afterthought public spaces; disconnected or skinny sidewalks; and mass-produced, generic neighborhoods surround us. We are destroying our landmarks, landscapes, environment, and history with new, but not necessarily better, development and public spaces. While our population is becoming more diverse, the public realms of our towns and cities across the country are becoming more homogenous, unauthentic, and uninteresting—"Anywhere, U.S.A." (Figures 1-1 and 1-2).

Figures 1-1 and 1-2. These are typical sights in most American communities, devoid of authenticity, uniqueness, and an attractive public realm.

The condition of our public spaces (e.g. sidewalks, plazas, parks, streets) often serves as a barometer of our communities' vitality, social cohesion, public health, sense of place, image, and identity. Because our own communities are not providing the special places that we need, as Howard Kunstler (in *Geography of Nowhere*) and innumerable others point out, we travel to places like Disneyland and other fantasy worlds to experience special public places (Figure 1-3). Most of us want more from our surroundings, and what we aren't getting in the public realm, we are creating in our private realms by personalizing our yards, our cars, and even our bodies in an attempt to highlight our uniqueness in a world of sameness (Figures 1-4 through 1-6).

Figure 1-3. Disneyland is one of many theme parks to which we escape the realities of our everyday lives in search of something (and someplace) better.

Figure 1-4. Residents in Chandler, Arizona, use unique fencing materials to both define their territory and convey their sense of pride.

Figure 1-5. Down the street in the same Chandler, Arizona, neighborhood, a household employs a high degree of creativity and resourcefulness to enhance their image—planted toilets as flowerpots.

Figure 1-6. Yard art is taken to extremes in order to satisfy one individual's desire to create a strong sense of place in this Oxnard, California, neighborhood.

Figures 1-7 and 1-8. Even hamlets of the smallest sizes are working hard to make the most of what they have—Welcome to Downtown Otis, Oregon.

Placemaking on a Budget (POAB) has emerged in response to the growing number of "placeless" spaces and projects. POAB is based on the premise that it is possible to enhance our community identity and increase real social connections to one another through improving our public realm, and that this can be accomplished largely through local resources, involved people, and creative thinking.

The past two decades have given rise to several paradigm shifts in community development philosophies—entitled Livable Communities, Smart Growth, New Urbanism, among others. These philosophies seek to regain a people-centered (as opposed to automobile-dominated) value system for development and redevelopment that emphasizes the role public spaces play in nurturing the well-being of people. These movements are gaining momentum across the country and are influencing many communities, large and small, to independently undertake community-based planning and design efforts that tap the connections between people and between people and place (Figures 1-7 and 1-8). POAB can be viewed as another step forward in this new community development paradigm, through which people can gain lost ground on their connections to community—and to each other—and work together to enhance their public realm.

USING PLACEMAKING ON A BUDGET

POAB is about creating meaningful places for people by people and empowering communities to develop great places in which to be—authentic places that reinforce local pride and identity. To help accomplish this, this PAS Report has been written to appeal to people of all backgrounds, to apply at any time, and to assist any community no matter what the geographical location or context. It is intended to benefit every member of a community (e.g. downtown merchants, students, business leaders, public agency staff, public officials, neighborhood leaders) and every type of community (e.g. rural, small town, suburban, urban) that seeks positive, meaningful change (Figure 1-9).

COMMON OBSTACLES TO PLACEMAKING

When a community is considering a placemaking project, a number of obstacles (real or perceived) may be expressed by peers or public officials who challenge project viability. Common reasons cited for limited opportunity for success may include:

- Lack of money
- Overburdened public agencies
- Disadvantaged economy
- Absence of local talent
- Excessive "red tape"
- Too few involved citizenry
- Sense of hopelessness
- Blighted environment

While these or other obstacles may seem to merit a pessimistic outlook for future potential, it is the innate belief of POAB that "each community boasts a unique combination of assets upon which to build its future" (Kretzmann and McKnight 1993). When seeking to uplift the qualities of a place, it is essential that communities organize their placemaking processes based on the concept of means and ends. When "means" (e.g. constrained financial resources, limited political support) are presented as overemphasized obstacles at the outset of a placemaking process, morale, energy, and hope of those involved can dwindle; conversely, when "ends" (e.g. visions of a desirable future, a project idea) are maintained as the focus of the beginning stages of placemaking processes, community members often adopt a visionary "what can be" perspective and quickly employ "can do" creative solutions to any obstacles.

Figure 1-9. Just a few minutes away from Otis, Oregon, residents of Lincoln City, Oregon, celebrate a community-based placemaking project that now serves as a source of local pride and inspiration.

To help POAB readers create the type of community or public space desired, this handbook is organized into four interrelated chapters that tell a story of the many ways to create place with very limited resources. Building upon the principle of Ready-Aim-Fire (Figure 1-10), Chapters 1 and 2 represent the "Ready" dimensions of placemaking; chapter 3, the "Aim" dimension; and chapter 4, the "Fire" dimension.

- Chapter 1 illustrates the importance of placemaking and provides a discussion of how *Placemaking on a Budget* is intended to benefit and be used by communities.

- Chapter 2 provides two approaches, along with examples, to identifying good placemaking projects, based on "community values" and "community canvases," that work to improve the vitality of the public realm and the connection of people to it.

- Chapter 3 centers on understanding the resources available to implement placemaking projects, including the importance of local volunteers and partnerships, as well as leveraging resources that are too often left untapped.

- Chapter 4 focuses on implementation and presents organizing techniques to make achieving placemaking objectives easier and more straightforward by answering the key questions of "who, what, when, where, why, how, and how much."

We hope that the framework, concepts, examples, and ideas contained with *Placemaking on a Budget* are both useful and inspiring to you and your community.

Placemaking on a Budget relies on uplifting the image and vitality of communities based on tapping authentic community attributes rather than replicating or transplanting ideas from other places—communities that adopt the "Anywhere, U.S.A.," approach often find themselves without the attributes that foster a sustainable sense of pride and identity.

CHAPTER 2

Identifying Meaningful Projects

f you agree that we *can* and *should* be doing a much better job of building a sense of community and place, where do we start? We must start at the fundamental level of connecting people and place—the health and vitality of any community is directly tied to residents' level of individual and collective connection to it. Arriving at this sense of local ownership can best be achieved by identifying the values of past and present generations as they are presented through a community's architecture, infrastructure, and landscape (the community's "canvases") and then expressing those values in new or amended canvases. Through these canvases, communities can enrich the experience of place by integrating dimensions of local history and culture, natural environment, and other unique community attributes into the public realm where they currently don't exist. It is important, therefore, to understand both a community's values and to recognize the plethora of readily available canvases within a community. Much like yin and yang, community values and community canvases are dependent upon each other when you are planning to do Placemaking on a Budget (Figure 2-1).

COMMUNITY VALUES AND CANVASES

Community Values

- History and culture (e.g., community leaders, past events)

- Natural environment (e.g., geology, flora, fauna, climate)

- Community attributes (e.g., traditions, local industry, points of pride)

Community Canvases

- Architecture (e.g., buildings, walls, other physical structures)

- Infrastructure (e.g., sidewalks, lights, benches, utilities)

- Landscape (e.g., parks, gardens, plantings, open space)

THE TWO APPROACHES TO MAKING PLACEMAKING ON A BUDGET A REALITY

There are two main ways to put the Placemaking on a Budget (POAB) model into action. One approach is to first identify community values and then identify potential canvases. The other approach is to identify the canvases first and the community values second. In reality, the two POAB approaches often occur simultaneously or in a continuous back-and-forth pattern.

The Community Values-based Approach

When using the community values-based approach, identify POAB projects by first exploring your local history and culture, natural environment, and community attributes. Understand what it is that makes your city, town, downtown, neighborhood, or district distinct—what sets it apart from other places. This includes discovering the unique and common talents, skills, industries, resources, and abilities found in the community. The appropriate canvas or canvases can then be identified to communicate these community values. This approach is most applicable if your community is initiating a planning process with a visioning component or if your community may not have a full appreciation for how special and unique it is.

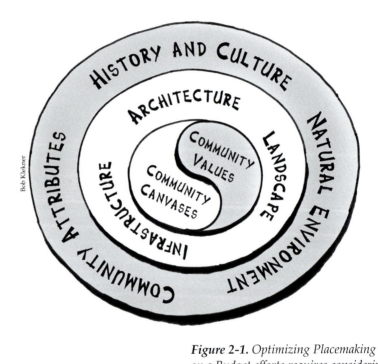

Figure 2-1. Optimizing Placemaking on a Budget efforts requires considering community values and community canvases as integral elements of projects—much like the interrelated nature of yin and yang.

The Community Canvases-based Approach

When using the community canvases-based approach, first inventory or pinpoint the potential canvases in your community, and then explore the realm of possible community values that can be conveyed through these canvases. This approach may be most relevant if your community is already planning to undertake a project (e.g., streetscape improvement, vacant lot enhancement, park development) and it is seeking opportunities to integrate expressions of community values as an added but essential dimension of the project.

The POAB project examples and ideas in this chapter are presented in both a community-values context and a community-canvas context. The examples highlighted here come from communities in which we have worked, where we have visited, as well as those we have learned about through examples submitted to us because people want to share their unique placemaking projects. We hope the discussion and illustrations provided in this chapter will inspire other communities to generate their own unique placemaking ideas.

COMMUNITY VALUE-BASED PROJECTS

As already noted, Placemaking on a Budget is not about big, flashy projects. It is about touching people by developing projects they can relate to and ones that mean something to them, make them smile, and make them feel good. In order to do this, it is necessary to understand their values as well as to involve them in creating and building the projects themselves. This section briefly describes the community values of history and culture, natural environment, and community attributes and then illustrates POAB projects inspired by these local community values.

Highlighting History and Culture

History and culture are likely the most commonly cherished community values. Residents often cite their memories of past events, civic leaders, and local heroes, of buildings no longer standing, or of a former business they patronized as a child. They will also talk about the native people who preceded them; the high school sport that always rallies the residents; the ethnicity or place of origin of those who helped settle the town; or the arts, music, dance, and theater found in the community today. Remember, conventional and traditional histories are not (and ideally, won't be) the only local stories to tell. Every community is distinct and offers something unique. Downtown Fort Bragg, California, for instance, in addition to being home to Coastal Redwoods and the historic Skunk Train, also boasts the unusual distinction of being home to a Tattoo History Museum (Figure 2-4).

Figure 2-2. Old boats are recycled as interesting docks that reinforce the area's nautical past along the waterfront in Melk, Austria.

Figure 2-3. Elements of the Vienna, Austria, historic drainage system are preserved and shared with the community against a modern backdrop.

Figure 2-4. Downtown Fort Bragg, California, boasts the unusual distinction of being home to a Tattoo History Museum.

Figure 2-5. Rather than place an old fire station bell in a museum, Escoloar, California, created a simple monument along a downtown street to inform the passersby of what once was.

Figure 2-6. Even in urban environments like Milwaukee, Wisconsin, communities can provide connections to their pre-automobile past. Here, hoofprints act as a wayfinding guide.

Celebrating history through interpretive signs. Traditional expressions of history and culture in the public realm include commemorative markers, plaques, or signs on important buildings or sites. While certainly attractive, such historic markers need not be expensive bronze engravings; instead, start simple. Find old photographs of important buildings or locations, and ask knowledgeable building owners or local history buffs to provide a brief description of the image. Display both items in the building's window to be enjoyed by all who pass by, as done in Bonners Ferry, Idaho (Figure 2-7). No need to wait for funds when paper can have the same impact. Or in the case of Cannon Beach, Oregon, interesting sites are marked with attractive, heavy plastic plaques (Figure 2-8). If grants, funds, or a desire eventually exists, graduate to professional bronze building plaques, as illustrated in Figure 2-9, in downtown Flagstaff, Arizona. Innumerable other examples exist that illustrate the use of interpretive signs to celebrate history (Figures 2-10 to 2-12).

Figure 2-7. In storefronts in downtown Bonners Ferry, Idaho, businesses tell historic stories of their buildings and important community events through poster board window displays that include photocopied photographs and typed accounts written by community members.

Figure 2-8. Simple and inexpensive interpretive signs can help tell the story of historical uses of buildings and sites as well as add meaning for those who live in or visit a community, such as this plastic plaque demarcating an historical site in Cannon Beach, Oregon.

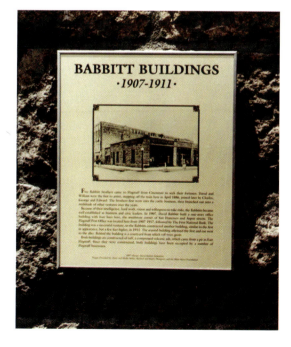

Figure 2-9. Adding value to the experience of place can be accomplished simply through wall plaques that tell the story of buildings, such as the Babbitt Building in downtown Flagstaff, Arizona.

Figure 2-10. While the beautiful courthouse building originally located at this Corvallis, Oregon, site is no longer standing, a simple photographic essay allows residents and visitors alike to admire the former structure.

Figure 2-11. Likewise, humorous dimensions of a community's history can be celebrated through the use of interpretive signs, such as this building's historic role as the gossip center in Cannon Beach, Oregon.

Figure 2-12. Recognizing unusual dimensions of a community's history is important to the identity of a place, such as the Mt. Healthy, Ohio, remembrance of its role as a refuge from the cholera epidemic. in 1850.

Using historical photographs for inspiration and ideas. The emotion underlying the individual and collective connections with history and culture also adds to the rich potential for conceiving and creating community value-based placemaking projects. Historic photographs and images often engender very strong feelings and ideas. For example, at a community meeting in Tonopah, Nevada, a small rural town working to rediscover its "heart," a resident brought in an old photograph showing the festive dances that used to take place in the middle of the street (Figure 2-13). While street dances are no longer possible because the old town road is now a busy state highway, a rich community dialogue ensued in which they determined that an underused parking lot could become the site for town dances through a few simple enhancements (Figures 2-14 and 2-15). In addition to photographs, historic postcards often inspire placemaking projects (Figure 2-16).

Figure 2-13. Tonopah, Nevada, is a former mining community that had a rich history of strong social events, including downtown street dances.

Figure 2-14. A parking lot in the center of downtown Tonopah, Nevada, was identified by the community as an ideal location for a flexible space that could serve as a parking lot and as a town plaza for community gatherings, including dances.

Figure 2-15. Through an understanding of community values, and by tapping the talents of local artists and tradespersons, the Tonopah community envisions the parking lot as a newfound place to celebrate and build community.

Figure 2-16. Even old postcards of legendary community features, such as the "Fountain of Youth" in St. Petersburg, Florida, can serve as local resources for identifying placemaking projects.

Genuine Curteich—Chicago. From the collection of Dr. M. Madilene Veverka and Vlasta Nosek Gufrey.

A GLIMPSE BACK IN TIME HIGH UPON A HILL: SIGNAL HILL, CALIFORNIA

Signal Hill, California, a 2.2-square-mile community in Los Angeles County has a rich history spanning from the time the area served as the homeland of the Puva Indians in the 1500s to, more recently, when oil was struck in 1921 and economic prosperity came. Atop its namesake hill, the city built a park that includes a series of vertical panels with windows emphasizing what once was and what is. Each panel's window frames a view of the community and surrounding areas as they are seen today. To remind visitor's of the area's history, each panel is stained with a silhouette and the ground below is painted with a sepia-toned "shadow" reflecting what the view would have been in earlier years.

Figure 2-18. Peering through a panel's window reveals a framed view of the present-day community and surrounding areas.

Figure 2-17. A series of panels in a Signal Hill park creates a simple focal point for visitors to learn about the community's history.

Figure 2-19. A "shadow" (stained into the concrete) of the panel and its window convey an image of what people may have seen from the very same vantage point in the early part of the community's history.

HARLEM GATEWAY PROJECT: NEW YORK, NEW YORK

New York City's Department of Transportation and Department of Design and Construction have implemented the Harlem Gateway streetscape enhancement project in an effort to refurbish the neighborhood's southern entrance. "Heritage Fixtures"—streetlights that include a map of the area and display portraits and brief biographical descriptions of famous Harlem residents—were designed by Holzman Pfeiffer Associates, Architects and Cline Bettridge Bernstein Lighting Design in partnership with Cityscape Institute, a program of the Central Park Conservancy. The Heritage Fixtures will be located along Central Park North (110th Street) between Fifth Avenue and Frederick Douglass Boulevard (8th Avenue) and will provide identity for different parts of the neighborhood as well as serve as one element in establishing 110th Street as a pedestrian-friendly environment. Figures 2-20 through 2-23 illustrate the prototype fixtures and attached sample plaques installed at Malcolm X Plaza located at Central Park North (110th St) and Lenox Avenue.

Figures 2-20 to 2-23. "Heritage Fixtures"—streetlights that include a map of the area and display portraits and brief biographical descriptions of famous Harlem, New York, residents—are a central part of the Harlem Gateway project.

All photos courtesy of John T. Reddick, Central Park Conservancy/Cityscape Institute

CASE STUDY 2.1

THE DOWNTOWN ENUMCLAW, WASHINGTON, STREETSCAPE ENCHANCEMENT PROJECT

By Les Johnson

Enumclaw, Washington, is east of Tacoma in the Puget Sound region. Historically, Enumclaw provided a regional commerce focus and provided many jobs in timber or agricultural industries. Virtually all purchasing of goods and services was conducted downtown. Since 1990, Enumclaw's economic base has changed: job rich industries have since gone, most residents now commute to urban areas for employment, and the city has become a bedroom community. These changes reduced the health of downtown businesses.

Project description. During the mid 1990s, the city began a planning effort that resulted in an Economic Development Action Plan (EDAP). The plan created a list of priorities for improving the economic condition of downtown. In response to the EDAP, the community specifically developed a plan to implement actions that would enhance the downtown. It included nine projects aimed at helping the community accomplish the "bigger purpose" of emphasizing that downtown provides an important civic space, the historical heart, the principal site for commerce, and a residential environment for the community. Based on the community's vision, the Downtown Enumclaw Streetscape Enhancement Project was earmarked as the first project to be implemented.

In July 2001, the city, the chamber of commerce, and the Enumclaw Downtown Partnership (the project team) selected a consulting team through an intensive community-based process to assist the community in the development of the downtown streetscape program. By April 2002, the concept and its related cost estimates were presented to the community. Based on the input received, the project and consulting teams refined the streetscape concept plan (Figure 2-24) and cost estimates. Subsequent steps included the preparation of construction documentation and initiation of the construction management process. The goal was to have the Cole Street portion of the Downtown Enumclaw Streetscape Program completed by the end of summer 2003.

Project results. The task of developing and recreating a "sense of place" within an enervated downtown was monumental. Value-added dimensions of the streetscape design that connected with important community values included:

- angled scoring on the concrete sidewalk to reflected the "String and Pole Yard" planting pattern for hops historically found within Enumclaw's agricultural fields;

- locally quarried Wilkeson (light gray/white in color) and Tenino (charcoal gray in color) sandstone served as the inspiration for a two-foot-wide basket weave pattern—called the chain pattern and used by the Salish Indians who once inhabited the region—demarcating the sidewalk environment from on-street parking (Figure 2-25); and

- heavy tubular metal benches reflected the truss structures of the flumes that once conveyed timber from area forests to the local sawmill, and the slats for the bench seats were made from cedar, an important natural resource to the region (Figure 2-26).

A vital component of this effort was project funding. The community-based design process of the downtown streetscape project contributed to the willingness of property owners to financially support the project through the establishment of a local improvement district. Construction of the project was completed on schedule and within budget. The streetscape project has stirred interest among multiple business owners who want to improve their façades and signage. Without question, the effort has brought about a new downtown focus and interest that has already positively changed the Enumclaw community.

Chapter 2. Identifying Meaningful Projects   21

Figure 2-24: Downtown Enumclaw's streetscape project, as defined by the community, was captured through a vision poster that conveyed not only design details but also the community values that underlie each.

Figure 2-25. The built sidewalks in downtown Enumclaw provide important connections to the community's agricultural and cultural heritage, as well as its geology.

Figure 2-26. The bench design for downtown Enumclaw integrates two important elements of the community's logging industry and surrounding forests—the cedar top and supporting truss structure.

Using Elements of the Natural Environment

The geographical setting of every community provides a web of natural features unique to that particular location on earth. The geology, climate, plants, animals, bodies of water, topography, and nighttime skies are among the many facets of the natural environment that help make every community different than any other. Most residents have strong connections with the natural environment, either through acts of God (e.g., earthquakes, tornadoes, or floods); changes in the seasons (e.g., summer brings sunshine, winter brings snow, or the annual migration of whales); personal hobbies (e.g., hiking, gardening, or weather watching); or the community setting itself (e.g., the surrounding Sonoran desert or the picturesque glacial valley). For many reasons, the natural environment itself or elements borrowed from it often play important roles in the development of placemaking projects.

Using the weather. Lincoln City, Oregon, is in the process of developing the Oregon Coast Weather Center, which capitalizes on its unique (sometimes perceived as negative) weather conditions in a project that has the entire community and state and federal agencies very involved and excited. The center was conceived during a planning process for Lincoln City's Village of Taft Redevelopment Plan. The original idea, which was voiced by a member of the local media and a Lincoln City resident, was to erect a rain gauge at the end of Southwest 51st Street to provide a point of interest for residents and visitors alike. That idea quickly blossomed into one for an educational and research center focused on weather and tsunamis, coupled with a museum showcasing weather- and tsunami-related artifacts and history. Not only will the center be an anchor project to increase the economic vitality of Lincoln City and the State of Oregon, but it wll also serve as a location to gather critical weather information to assist with coastal tsunami warnings, weather forecasting, and weather and seismic studies (Figures 2-27 and 2-28). In addition to Lincoln City, other places throughout the world draw inspiration from the weather to add interest and meaning to their public areas and built environments (Figures 2-29 through 2-32).

Figure 2-27. Throughout time, the Siletz Bay in Lincoln City, Oregon, and the Pacific Ocean provided people with a setting of inspiration and dynamic weather conditions, as well as natural resource assets for recreation, commerce, and industry.

Figure 2-28. At the west end of Southwest 51st Street—Lincoln City, Oregon's, most popular point of beach access—the community has secured a site for its envisioned Oregon Coast Weather Center.

Figure 2-29. In Eastern Europe, identifying high-water marks from floods provides a way to not only document environmental history, but also to create an interesting pedestrian feature.

Figure 2-30. Taking advantage of its climate and creative citizenry, Palm Springs, California, has constructed bus stops throughout the community that rely on the sun to power the lights for nighttime transit riders.

Figure 2-31. Extremely cold weather during the winter in Fairbanks, Alaska, is combined with the talents of artists to create ice sculptures that are located throughout the downtown streetscape.

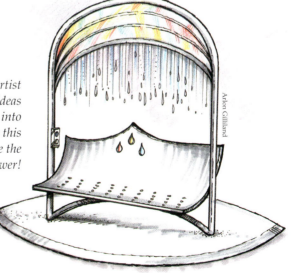

Figure 2-32. Lincoln City, Oregon, artist Arlon Gilliland transforms the creative ideas brainstormed by residents and merchants into playful and realistic renderings—like this rain bench that allows seated visitors to be the recipients of their very own rain shower!

Figure 2-33. Celebrating natural hazards, such as the San Andreas Earthquake Fault in San Juan Bautista, California, helps educate the public as well as provides points of interest and intrigue.

Using geology. We often overlook the most interesting natural elements of our community's natural environment—geologic features—because they are beneath our feet! In San Juan Bautista, California, for example, where the San Andreas Fault runs along the edge of the small town, the community has a monument denoting this fact and developed an interpretive "Earthquake Walk" that at one time also included a meter monitoring the activity of the fault (Figure 2-33). Many other communities tap their geologic attributes to add to their placemaking efforts (Figures 2-34 through 2-38).

Figure 2-34. Geologic hazards, such as earthquakes, can serve as sources of inspiration for the design of public plazas, such as the faultline represented in Los Angeles's Pershing Square.

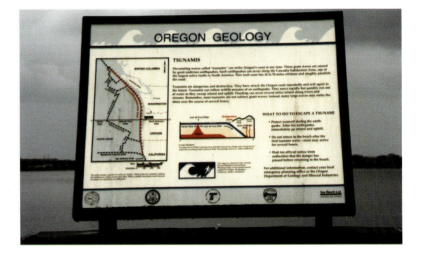

Figure 2-35. Telling the story of an area's natural resources adds to the connection between people and place, such as this interpretive sign describing the relationship between geology and tsunamis at a roadside stop in Oregon.

Figure 2-36. Taking full advantage of their abundant natural resources, Melk, Austria, sells local rocks and gems to interested visitors.

Figure 2-37. Informing downtown visitors of the Grand Canyon's geology, while providing a meaningful piece of public art to locals, is what Flagstaff, Arizona, accomplished in its downtown.

Figure 2-38. In downtown Sacramento, California, the community pays tribute to the major environmental zones of the state through public art, including the use of sandstone from the Pacific Coast and quartzite from California's Central Valley.

Using flora and fauna. The plants and animals found within and around communities are often seized as sources of placemaking inspiration because of their obvious and readily visible nature. Figures 2-39 through 2-44 provide examples of how flora and fauna can influence project ideas in communities.

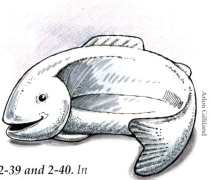

Figures 2-39 and 2-40. In Lincoln City, Oregon, artist Arlon Gilliland transformed creative ideas brainstormed by residents and merchants into playful but realistic renderings of a fish bench and a seaweed and sand dollar gateway sign, which reflect attributes of the local environment.

Figure 2-41. A logo developed by the community can reinforce the identity of a place, such as this fish logo installed on a handsome trash container in Roseburg, Oregon.

Figure 2-42. Environmental features of historic importance to communities can be derived from old postcards, such as the orange crops and snow-capped mountains in California.

C.T. Art – Colortone. From the collection of Dr. M. Madilene Veverka and Vlasta Gufrey

Figures 2-43 and 2-44. In State College, Pennsylvania, the community pays its respect for pigs and other farm animals that once roamed the downtown streets.

Figures 2-46 through 2-47. The Los Angeles River Murals, Paramount, California. Three large murals, which feature groups of sea turtles, Orcas, and sharks with orange Garibaldi, adorn the levee of the Los Angeles River in Paramount, California. The city partnered with artist Adel Rakhshani, the Los Angeles County Public Works Department, and the U.S. Army Corps of Engineers to complete the water-themed paintings.

All photos courtesy of City of Paramount, California

Using Community Attributes Other than History, Culture, and the Environment

Not all the unique features, characteristics, or values of a community will fall under the history and culture or natural environment categories. It is essential to explore and tap all potential community attributes to develop placemaking projects with long-term community ownership. Every community possesses skills, talents, interests, imagination, creativity, and occupations as plentiful and diverse as the number of residents. Unique community attributes are important—yet are often unknown, forgotten, or untapped resources and inspiration for developing meaningful placemaking projects. Involve community members to uncover what makes your town, neighborhood, or district different from other places. You may be surprised by what you learn.

Seeing your community through the eyes of your young people. Many communities exhibit their strong commitment to young people by employing children's artistic skills to create community-based art, including tiles for walls and sidewalks, as well as other "canvases" within the community. In San Gabriel, California, classrooms of talented fourth graders painted tiles that are major features in gateway walls and along sidewalks throughout the Mission District (Figure 2-48). Other placemaking projects exhibiting a commitment to young people's interpretation of community values on a variety of community canvases (see Figures 2-49 through 2-55) include the Oklahoma City, Oklahoma, National Memorial chalkboards, the Prescott Valley, Arizona, rock, and the Pampa, Texas, art history wall.

Figure 2-48. Wall tiles painted by youth not only add to visual interest and community ownership but also—as in San Gabriel, California—serve as a special gateway element to welcome people into the community.

Figure 2-49. This low-income, ethnically diverse San Diego neighborhood commercial district celebrates its commitment to youth through murals on the façade of a childcare center.

Figures 2-50 and 2-51. Youth graffiti is art in Prescott Valley, Arizona. Graffiti rock, located at the front of the high school, displays ever-changing works of art that are enjoyed by the entire community.

Figure 2-52. The Oklahoma City National Memorial invites youth activity through its ground-level chalkboards.

Figure 2-53. Children can be active participants in transforming blank walls into visually interesting and meaningful architectural elements, such as this wall on the campus of Washington School in Glendora, California.

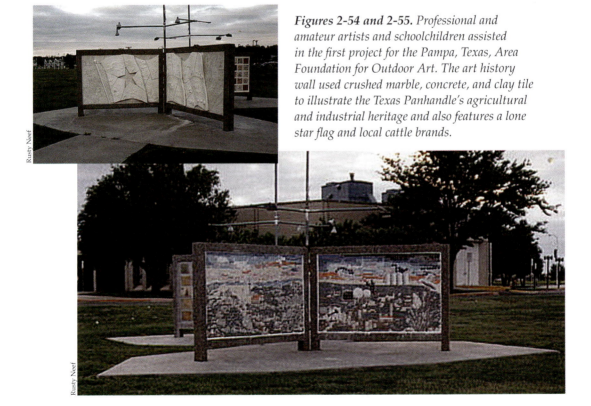

Figures 2-54 and 2-55. Professional and amateur artists and schoolchildren assisted in the first project for the Pampa, Texas, Area Foundation for Outdoor Art. The art history wall used crushed marble, concrete, and clay tile to illustrate the Texas Panhandle's agricultural and industrial heritage and also features a lone star flag and local cattle brands.

Local industry influences sense of place. What people do—or once did—for a living is often an important topic of conversation in communities. Local industries, businesses, and trades can be used to inspire meaning and significance in the public realm (Figures 2-56 through 2-58).

Figures 2-56 and 2-57. Creating a first impression at a community entrance was accomplished by Cashmere, Washington, through the use of simple visual ties to its apple-related agrarian heritage.

Figure 2-58. In downtown Chattanooga, Tennessee, local masons and artists combine their talents to create public art celebrating the community's brick-making heritage.

Community icons and local personalities. While gossip about people may be a favorite pastime in many communities, it is often those colorful people who are remembered in the public realm (Figures 2-59 through 2-61).

Figure 2-59. The restaurant Eleanor's Undertow, a Lincoln City, Oregon, institution, puts its signature on a new waterfront sidewalk with this jeweled mermaid—an icon that is reflective of the spirited nature of the restaurant owner.

Figure 2-60. A memorial to a local celebrity can help a community remember an important part of its heritage, such as this statue of the Laguna Beach, California, Greeter—a person who dedicated his days to making people feel welcomed in this community.

Figure 2-61. Remembering residents and merchants of yesteryear who contributed to the community in unique ways is what Sterling, Colorado, did for its most famous popcorn proprietor.

Placemaking through dogs and other pets. Man's best friend often inspires (or necessitates) placemaking elements in communities throughout the world. Figures 2-62 through 2-64 demonstrate simple and fun ways to accommodate dogs in the public realm, as well as add interest to passersby.

Figure 2-62 (left). *Examples of dog leash tie-ups outside of stores in Vienna, Austria.*
Figure 2-63 (right). *Here is a "dog parking" spot on a building façade in Sicily, Italy.*

Figure 2-64. *Drinking fountains, a common element in public spaces, can have greater meaning when they consider dogs, such as this one in Laguna Beach, California.*

Combining placemaking and community information systems. People appreciate being informed about goings-on in their community, as well as being oriented about where they are. Through unique approaches to signage and bulletin boards, community information can be displayed while contributing to a more interesting visual environment (Figures 2-65 through 2-69).

Figure 2-65. This community bulletin board in downtown Chapel Hill, North Carolina, not only adds to the sense of place but also informs people of events and services.

Figure 2-67. Recessed doorways to storefronts, such as this one in Flagstaff, Arizona, are ideal locations for community bulletin boards, providing passersby with information and exposing merchants to potential consumers.

Figure 2-66. Cloverdale, California, provides a simple bulletin board in its downtown for posting notices of community activities.

Figure 2-68. Combining a blank wall with a community's need for information on goings-on is what Mendocino, California, does to keep in the know.

Figure 2-69. A simple sign can be enhanced through creative painting, such as the pencil signposts in Mt. Healthy, Ohio.

Using street furniture to tell the story. Figures 2-70 and 2-71 show how street furniture can be used to enhance the experience of place.

Figures 2-70 and 2-71. *Scottish designer Mil Stricevic created the Sonic Vista, a bench with a built-in solar-powered MP3 audio player that plays recordings specific to the location. In Barrow-in-Furrow, United Kingdom, residents have the opportunity to decide on content for the benches.*

COMMUNITY CANVAS-BASED PROJECTS

Learn to see everything as a potential canvas on which to convey community values and create more meaningful places. We generally sort the range of possible canvases into three categories: architecture, infrastructure, and landscape. The expression of community values through these canvases taps the multiple senses of people (e.g., touch, sight, sound, smell) and reinforces a connection to the community's past, present, or future. These canvases are often readily available for little or no expense, or are typical expenditures of the community (e.g., public improvements) to which value can be added.

Architecture

The architecture of your community serves as a very powerful canvas. Begin to look at buildings and structures in your community with a new eye—see the many opportunities they present. As the following examples illustrate, there are a plethora of ways to use architecture as a canvas.

Façades, building walls, and fences. As shown in Figures 2-72 through 2-88, blank or underused façades and building walls offer a large community canvas for murals, artwork, and more—don't forget to be daring with the façades fronting on alleys as they are natural canvases for very creative and exciting POAB projects.

Figure 2-72. Sometimes silly signs can be added to the blank walls of buildings to remind us of our surroundings, such as this sky sign in San Francisco, California.

Figure 2-73. Parking structures can be transformed from dull, monolithic elements of the urban environment, as shown by this Portland, Oregon, parking garage with its upper stories of hanging fish.

Figure 2-74. A super-sized painted wall sign in Portland, Oregon, both advertises a business and enhances the surrounding visual environment.

Figure 2-75. Many communities, such as Covington, Louisiana, use blank building walls as backdrops for performing arts or as screens for outdoor summer movies.

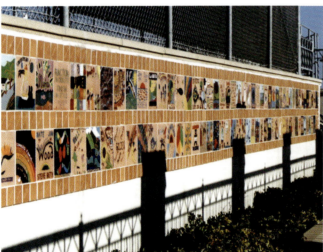

Figure 2-76. Wall tiles painted by children, such as these in Laguna Beach, California, add great meaning and community ownership to places.

Figure 2-77. A blank wall in Prosser, Washington, provides an opportune canvas to paint a snapshot of the community's history for all to enjoy.

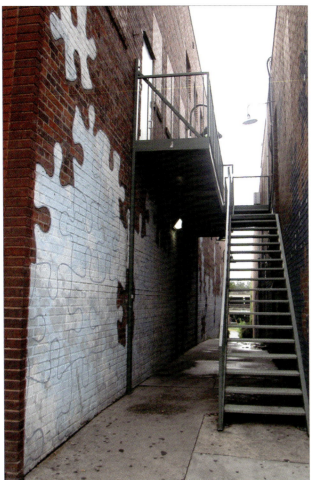

Figure 2-78. *The jigsaw puzzle pieces painted on these otherwise barren walls in Chapel Hill, North Carolina, enliven the narrow space between buildings and invite pedestrian traffic.*

Figure 2-79. *Simple enhancements to a rear entrance help create "place" in this alley environment in Escolar, California.*

Figure 2-80. *By paying special attention to rear entrances, this alley environment in Chattanooga, Tennessee, is transformed into an inviting space.*

Figure 2-81. Painted wall signs can add creativity and needed information to an otherwise blank side of a building, such as this alley signage in Orange, California.

Figure 2-82. Unarticulated walls can be transformed into a seemingly vital part of the building through artistic interpretation of architectural features, such as found in downtown Fort Worth, Texas (the blank wall is on the right).

Figure 2-84. With or without the sun, these painted palm tree shadows create unique scenes in Phoenix, Arizona.

Figure 2-83. These otherwise underused alley walls in Santa Fe, New Mexico, are home to display cases for art and merchandise.

Figure 2-85. A well-known bookstore in Portland, Oregon, added value to the public realm by transforming an external structural column into a stack of books.

Figure 2-86. In downtown Redding, California, a mural reminds pedestrians and drivers of California's redwood forests.

Figure 2-87. Fences, an important architectural element of our communities for screening, security, and defining boundaries, can also be creative features, like this one in Kansas City, Missouri.

Figure 2-88. An eclectic fence designed by a local artist softens a vacant lot between two buildings in Globe, Arizona.

THE LINCOLN CITY, OREGON, HISTORIC FINGER

Figure 2-89. *The historic Village of Taft, Lincoln City, Nebraska.*

Many communities have a state highway as their downtown's main street. The main street of Lincoln City, Oregon, is Highway 101. Since state highway standards are often more stringent and less flexible than those of municipalities, many communities and businesses along state highways find themselves challenged to accomplish even the most routine objectives. Within the Village of Taft in Lincoln City, local businesses along Highway 101 were prevented from having any signage that projected beyond the front façade of their building—this space was subject to the strict standards of the Oregon Department of Transportation. A community member turned to a historic photograph (Figure 2-89) to overcome this obstacle—painted wall signs to the rescue! Now the Village of Taft and all of Lincoln City have newfound opportunities to direct people to points of interest throughout the community (Figure 2-90).

Figure 2-90. *The Village of Taft today, with the painted wall sign.*

Doors and windows. Using building doors and windows as a canvas can transform a space and provide a new location to celebrate the community (Figures 2-91 through 2-98).

Figures 2-91 and 2-92. *Inexpensive playground equipment and brightly painted pictures on boarded-up windows transform this vacant, neglected parcel into a wonderful space for children in this Cincinnati, Ohio, inner-city neighborhood.*

Figure 2-93. *The void created by blank utility doors was alleviated in downtown Fort Worth, Texas, through the use of creative faux-brick painting.*

Figures 2-94 and 2-95. *Kansas City, Missouri, demonstrates how boarded-up windows can be livened up by tapping the talents of local artists.*

Figure 2-96. A building's nooks and crannies can be tapped to serve many needs, such as this community bulletin board located in a store's doorway in downtown Mendocino, California.

Figure 2-97. Security grilles become design features as illustrated in this Kansas City, Missouri, sporting goods storefront where oars have been used in place of traditional grilles.

Figure 2-98. In Cesky Krumlov in the Czech Republic, a building's window security grilles are designed as artwork that conveys a nighttime scene of the town with a starry sky.

HOLLYWOOD'S LIVELY ROLL-DOWN SECURITY DOORS

Figure 2-99

After residents noticed that roll-down security doors on Hollywood Boulevard businesses attracted graffiti and diminished the nightlife of Los Angeles's famous avenue, artist Susan Krieg and her team of muralists painted the likenesses of movie stars on 40 doors between September and October 2002 (Figures 2-99 through 2-101). The project was sponsored by the Hollywood Beautification Team and funded by the Los Angeles Community Redevelopment Agency. The group has attempted to match the portraits to the names along the Hollywood Walk of Fame and has taken requests from businesses.

Figure 2-100

Figure 2-101

Storefronts. Storefronts, such as those in Figures 2-102 through 2-106, can add color and life to your public spaces and can contribute to creating a unique character authentic to your community.

Figure 2-102. An area can be greatly enlivened just by adding a bit of color to a storefront, as evidenced in this New Orleans, Louisiana, example.

Figure 2-103. In Passau, Germany, a hand-painted planter box is used to enliven both the storefront and the commercial district.

Figure 2-104. This Laguna Beach, California, storefront illustrates how vitality can be added to the public realm through the use of multicolored tiles.

Chapter 2. Identifying Meaningful Projects   47

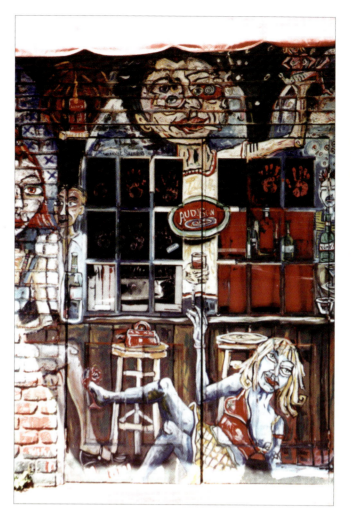

Figure 2-105. While storefront murals are not for every community, they can be easily implemented projects that contribute to the character of eclectic business districts, such as this "graffiti door" found in New Orleans, Louisiana.

Figure 2-106. A Hardy, Arkansas, business owner commissioned two artists to paint a mural representing five former landmarks: a railroad depot, gas station, bridge, inn, and elegant home. The owner wanted to provide a tribute to his hometown and to preserve part of its architectural heritage.

Figure 2-107. Nye Beach, Oregon, provides a reminder of opportunities to add value and meaning to everyday features, such as benches, through the stylistic addition of the community's name to the backrest.

Infrastructure

Canvases for placemaking projects abound in your community's infrastructure, most notably through the streetscape features and utilities. Some streetscape elements already exist in the public realm (e.g., bus shelters), and some are new elements that communities purchase (e.g., benches). If you are going to purchase these elements anyway, why not try to add meaning and community identity to them? Unfortunately, many of these opportunities are often overlooked, and the "Anywhere USA" image is proliferated. Don't let some of these easy ways to add meaning and creativity to your public realm pass your community by.

Street furniture. Capitalize on a planned streetscape program as an opportunity to tell the story of your community or draw upon individual elements, such as benches, streetlights, sidewalks, trash cans, bike racks, or bus shelters to highlight special attributes of your community (Figures 2-107 through 2-124).

Figure 2-108. Incorporating natural materials into utilitarian street furniture adds a unique dimension to public spaces, such as this rock bench in Laguna Beach, California.

Figure 2-109. A creative merchant in Laguna Beach, California, transformed a salvaged segment of curb and gutter into a storefront bench.

Figure 2-110. The backs of benches can be enlivened in many different ways, such as this decorative cityscape silhouette in Wenatchee, Washington.

Figures 2-111 and 2-112. Merging public art with sidewalk seating can inject whimsy and fun into the sidewalk environment, such as this shoe seat in the Mt. Adams district of Cincinnati, Ohio.

Figure 2-113. Seating can be designed to be both functional and to serve as a storyboard about a community, such as this mosaic covered bench in Houston, Texas.

Figure 2-114. Utilitarian bicycle racks can add value and interest to the sidewalk environment through creative metal work, such as this one in downtown Sacramento, California.

Figure 2-115. Trash receptacles can be tailored for the local environment using local materials, such as this rock trashcan in Cannon Beach, Oregon.

Figure 2-116. Along the sidewalks in Belmont Shores, California, parking meters cast creative "shadows," such as this leashed dog.

Figure 2-117. For communities whose sidewalks are not wide enough for outdoor dining, Mountain View, California, demonstrates how on-street parking spaces can be used as a flexible location for tables, chairs, and potted plants.

Figures 2-118 and 2-119. As illustrated in many European cities, lighting can be both a simple and inexpensive way to transform otherwise lifeless and uninteresting spaces, as shown in these Vienna, Austria, streets.

Figure 2-120. Bicycle parking in front of a Portland, Oregon, bookstore is made much more interesting by the bike-related book titles cut into header plates welded onto the bright red tubular steel racks.

Figures 2-121 and 2-122. *A Los Angeles Neighborhood Initiative group in the Byzantine-Latino Quarter employed the artistic talents of local schoolchildren in decorating sidewalk trash receptacles. The project not only tackled the neighborhood's trash problem but also helped strengthen collaboration within the community.*

Figure 2-123. *Grants Pass, Oregon, sought to bring public art into downtown by installing distinctive benches donated as memorials. The benches have designs celebrating local wildlife, recreation, and landmarks.*

Figure 2-124. *The nonprofit Downtown Long Beach Associates in Long Beach, California, sponsored the installation of bike racks individually tailored for downtown locations. The racks serve not only as a safe place for bicyclists to park their bikes but also as unique public art pieces that pay tribute to the local streetscape and architecture.*

Paths and walkways. The surfaces underneath our feet, hooves, paws, and wheels—such as sidewalks, streets, recreational surfaces, pathways—also offer opportunities for enhancing the meaning of the public realm (Figures 2-125 through 2-136).

Figure 2-126. *As found throughout New Orleans, Louisiana, imbedding the name of a street (current or original) into the sidewalk is an interesting way to identify the street, connect with history, and create pedestrian interest.*

Figure 2-125. *Milwaukee, Wisconsin, pays tribute to its cultural diversity through youth-designed tiles embedded in sidewalks.*

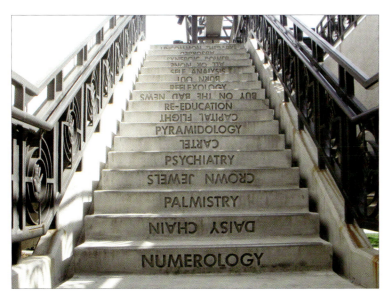

Figure 2-127. *The steps leading to this Los Angeles, California, light rail station do more than just convey the movement of people.*

Figure 2-128. *As Rancho Santa Fe, California, demonstrates, public staircases provide an excellent canvas upon which to add visual interest and cultural artwork.*

Figure 2-129. With just a little paint walking surfaces can take on new interest to pedestrians, such as these painted footsteps in Santa Fe, New Mexico.

Figure 2-130. Connections with the grape-growing and winemaking heritage of Windsor, California, are achieved through special imprints in the community's sidewalks.

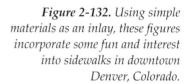

Figure 2-131. Chattanooga, Tennessee, integrates dance steps into the sidewalk—adding an element of fun and whimsy to this eclectic, artsy neighborhood.

Figure 2-132. Using simple materials as an inlay, these figures incorporate some fun and interest into sidewalks in downtown Denver, Colorado.

Figure 2-133. Fisherman's Wharf in San Francisco, California, includes artistic sidewalk inlays that highlight the historic Barbary Coast Trail.

Figures 2-134 and 2-135. Allowing youth to create the spaces where they recreate is an essential ingredient for building community ownership, such as Depoe Bay, Oregon's, skateboard park.

Figure 2-136. In Santa Barbara, California, one neighborhood entry is highlighted with monuments built of locally quarried stone.

KEEPING A COMMITMENT TO PUBLIC ART IN TEMPE, ARIZONA

Southern Arizona's rugged desert scenery has long served as an inspiration for artists and designers. Artists Scott Cisson, Niki Glen, Helen Helwig, and Joe Tyler, in conjunction with art students at Tempe's McClintock High School, continued this legacy when they drew from the region's landscape, climate, and artistic styles to create an unusual bus shelter at the school. The shelter, a sculpture entitled "The Elements," integrated the four ancient elements of earth, air, fire, and water. As shown in Figure 2-137, the artists employed steel, stone, copper, neon, and handmade ceramic tile to symbolize the elements, with imaginative components such as a movable roof and a copper sun.

Figure 2-137

The sculpture is only one of the many distinctive bus shelters around the city. The city of Tempe's Art in Transit program, which encourages residents to use the bus, bicycle, or walk, has helped sponsor 13 shelters, as well as bike lockers and racks, buses wrapped in art, and street and path improvements. "The Elements" was funded jointly by Art in Transit and the Municipal Arts Commission. The program is part of the city's larger attempt to support art in public and private spaces. In 1988, the city council passed an ordinance setting aside a portion of the capital improvement budget for art and three years later adopted an ordinance requiring public art in large private developments.

The dedication the artists had in creating an exceptional bus shelter is analogous to the commitment Tempe has made to public art, placemaking, and public transit. The Clean Air Campaign, a local organization that seeks to increase public awareness and participation in transit, honored the city's efforts to increase bus ridership and make transit a pleasurable experience for residents by giving "The Elements" its 2000 MAG Livable Communities Award. Certainly, the Art in Transit program has made a difference in how the residents of Tempe view both public transportation and their city.

Utilities. As illustrated in Figures 2-138 through 2-146, functional elements (e.g., utility boxes, electric substations, manhole covers, and construction barricades) provide readily available canvases upon which to celebrate our communities.

Figure 2-138. *With a little creativity, utility cabinets can be transformed into more visually interesting elements of the streetscape environment, as can be seen throughout Santa Fe, New Mexico.*

Figure 2-139. *The mermaids painted on this utility box in downtown Coronado, California, playfully highlight the area's ocean character. Local youth and artists painted this and several other utility boxes.*

Figure 2-140. *Utility cabinets have become an important part of the landscape design in this shopping center plaza in Houston, Texas.*

Figure 2-141. *Murals help to soften and add meaning to an otherwise potentially obtrusive community facility in this Santa Fe, New Mexico, neighborhood.*

Figure 2-142. Towns often seek ways to express their unique identities—a water tower in Kingsburg, California, is transformed into a teapot.

Figure 2-144. A few simple hand-painted flowers elevate this Regensburg, Germany, garbage dumpster from an eyesore to piece of public art.

Figure 2-143. Local artistic talent transformed a steam vent in downtown Fairbanks, Alaska, into a pleasant visual element.

Figures 2-145 and 2-146. Two public art projects in King County, Washington, have transformed ordinary water facilities into distinctive and appealing places. "Waterworks Gardens," a beautiful eight-acre stormwater treatment plant, has become a popular spot for weddings. "The Rain Drain," which is integrated into the North Creek Pump Station building, symbolizes the connection between nature and the built environment by directing rainwater through a sculpted copper drain.

Bridges. Bridges and freeway overpasses or underpasses are undertapped canvases that can not only connect people to one another physically, but can also visually link people to important community attributes. Figures 2-147 through 2-153 illustrate how communities capitalize upon bridges for their ability to serve as a POAB canvas.

Figure 2-147. Highway overpasses provide a highly visible canvas upon which to convey an area's connection to its environment and heritage, such as this overpass in the Pacific Northwest that integrates a scene with salmon swimming upstream in a river.

Figure 2-148. An autumn-themed design painted on this Austrian roadway overpass (between Linz and Salzburg) highlights the splendor of this region in the fall and creates a more interesting and personalized environment for passersby.

Figure 2-149. The rock base of this bridge spanning the Tennessee River in Chattanooga, Tennessee, is also used as a climbing wall for the community's outdoor enthusiasts.

Figure 2-150. Besides offering enhanced public safety, temporary construction barriers can be transformed into interim visual assets—such as these youth-painted barriers in Boston, Massachusetts.

Figures 2-151 and 2-152. Construction walls can contribute rather than detract from the visual experience, as illustrated in these examples from Vienna, Austria, and Denver, Colorado.

Figure 2-153. The Oceanside, California, Redevelopment Agency gave a new railroad undercrossing a distinctive "Oceanside Wave" theme suggesting the nearby shoreline. The crossing and adjoining plazas provide a lively link between downtown and the beach and pier.

Landscape. The landscape is a natural for a POAB canvas (no pun intended). Elements such as trees, flowers, and plantings can serve as canvases, as can monuments or gateways placed in our landscape. As Figures 2-154 through 2-164 demonstrate, there are many opportunities to explore ways in which your community can use its landscape to develop creative and meaningful projects.

Figure 2-154. Planters can be educational for all who pass by them when they include simple interpretive signage telling about the plants and who cares for them, such as this sidewalk planter in New York City, New York.

Figure 2-155. To enhance the sense of place and visual interest of communities, street trees, such as these in Santa Fe, New Mexico, can be selected for the color of their foliage.

Figure 2-156. Time and the persistent training of shrubbery yield a welcoming neighborhood entrance in Irvine, California.

Figure 2-157. In downtown Sacramento, California, the edge of a plaza is defined by landscaping in the form of a topiary of people standing arm-in-arm.

Figures 2-158 and 2-159. Trees themselves can be celebrated as important community assets and can be signed as part of a "tree tour," such as this Black Oak found in a Sacramento, California, park.

Figure 2-160. A simple picket fence can be transformed into a unique part of the landscape for all to enjoy, such as this colorful crayon fence in downtown Glendora, California.

Figure 2-161. Adding music to the public realm can greatly contribute to the positive feelings about a place and can be achieved without the use of unsightly audio speakers, such as this camouflaged landscape element in Houston, Texas.

Figure 2-162. Rather than removing an old gas pump, the Sherwood, Oregon, community transformed it into a community park, reminding the community of the way things used to be.

Figure 2-163. Celebrating the importance of birds to their community, Brookings, Oregon, residents build and proudly erect birdhouses for their aviary friends.

Figure 2-164. A simple community garden, such as this one in downtown Florence, Arizona, can do so much to not only visually enhance a neighborhood, but also bring neighbors together in a spirit of cooperation and community building.

MINING LANDSCAPE INSPIRES GATEWAYS
TONOPAH, NEVADA

Tonopah, Nevada, during an effort to revitalize its downtown, noted the need to establish special gateway treatments at each entry to town. Finding inspiration from its proud mining history and its rich geology, the community designed gateways using local stone as a base on which a heavy timber mining hoist would stand (mining hoists dot the hillsides of Tonopah and are recognized landmarks to residents and visitors alike). Several community members with the skills and materials needed to build these gateway features have been actively constructing them to benefit the sense of place and identity.

Figure 2-165

LIVING TREES IN STERLING, COLORADO

Sterling, Colorado, an agricultural and ranching community in the northeastern corner of the state, is known as the "City of Living Trees." Like most communities, Sterling routinely removes those trees in its parks and along its streets that have died. Over a decade ago, local artist Brad Rhea recognized an opportunity to transform the dead trees into "living trees" (meaning dead trees that provide vitality as cultural elements of the landscape) and community assets. With the community's support, Brad pursued his vision by carving the tree trunk and boughs into his first sculpture, "Skygrazers," of giraffes reaching to the sky (Figure 2-166). Since that initial sculpture, more than a dozen other trees have been carved with themes ranging from the "Butterfly" and the "Golfer" to the "Minute Man" and "Plainsman Pete." Recently, local organizations, businesses, and individuals have raised funds to create to-scale bronze replicas of two of the trees to preserve them from the weather in perpetuity. The "living trees" are symbols of community pride and contribute significantly to Sterling's local, regional, and national identity.

Figure 2-166

CASE 2.2 STUDY

THE REVIVAL OF CONFETTI PARK, NEW ORLEANS, LOUISIANA

By Blake Roberts

Like many playgrounds in New Orleans and other cities, Confetti Park was a frightening place for parents. Toddlers risked minor scrapes, cuts, and even severe injuries on the swings, metal bars, and slides. There was little protection from falls at the base of the equipment and one 12-foot-tall metal structure, termed the "Tower of Death," was dangerously high for children to climb. When the New Orleans Recreation Department (NORD) lacked sufficient funds for major changes, parents in the Algiers Point neighborhood finally felt that they needed to take action. As a result, a local fund-raising group, Confetti Kids, was born.

The organization took a number of tacks toward raising the money needed for refurbishing the park, including holding bake sales, garage sales, and a now annual benefit called Swing for Swings. Confetti Kids saw the value in partnering with government, businesses, and other nonprofit organizations. They created a cooperative agreement with NORD to renovate and maintain the playground. The Algiers Point city councilwoman has provided guidance in obtaining grants, and the Old Algiers Main Street program has co-sponsored Swing for Swings. The group also received donated materials from a local ship repair and construction company and a grant from KaBOOM!, a company that helps create custom-built playgrounds.

After two years of effort, work on Confetti Park was completed in October 2002 (Figures 2-166 through 2-169). According to Kristin Gisleson-Palmer, co-founder and president of Confetti Kids, local families have been successful in placing the neighborhood's stamp on the playground, particularly the park's appearance. The new play equipment complements Algiers Point's historic architecture. Confetti Kids hired Steve Kline, a local artist who had installed the distinctive "Confetti Fence" a decade earlier that gave the playground its nickname, to create benches and a gate.

Confetti Park and Confetti Kids are both now an important part of the neighborhood's quality of life. Gisleson-Palmer knows of two families who moved to Algiers Point largely because of the park. Confetti Kids is also involved in the planning of an additional neighborhood playground. Certainly, the organization's work has illustrated how residents can make a community liability an asset.

Figures 2-167, 2-168, and 2-169. The completed park and its many attractive elements.

UNDERSTANDING THE VALUES OF COMMUNITY AND PLACE

In POAB, the process is as important as the product—if not arguably more so. Providing ample opportunities for people to articulate what is most important to them about their community is a basic ingredient to both the community value-based and canvas-based approaches for identifying placemaking projects. To identify the most complete palette of POAB ideas, it is necessary to involve community members and engage them in a process that includes both observation and research. Ideas and values that yield the greatest level of community support often become the projects with the greatest chance of becoming on-the-ground realities. Through field observation—watching and listening without actually participating—a greater understanding of a community's history and culture, its natural environment, and other community attributes may surface. Similarly, simple research of the history, culture, environment, and people of a community will also generate many new and important POAB ideas. As articulated below, there are many meaningful ways to discover community values through community involvement, observation, and research.

PLACEMAKING IDEAS ORIGINATE FROM THE COMMUNITY

Often, in an effort to improve their vitality or image, communities will hire consultants to develop the "big ideas." If the hired professionals are performing their function responsibly, the ideas for placemaking projects will originate from community residents and will be appropriate to the local context. Consultants, then, should serve as facilitators who seek to extract ideas from the community and to add value to those ideas through their experience and skills. Communities undertaking visioning or placemaking efforts should be sure that community participation and involvement is an integral part of the process— successful and long-lived projects are truly owned by the community itself.

Figure 2-170

Figure 2-171

Community Involvement

Community involvement approaches that lead to listening, storytelling, and many other activities that can capture history and culture, the natural environment, and other community attributes include the following:

- Explore cultural values and history at community workshops
- Hold a culture and heritage fair
- Interview local elders
- Invite storytellers to attend local meetings
- Arrange for youth to research history and recreate it through art (song, dance, theatre, or physical forms)
- Interview local environmentalists and environmental organizations
- Brainstorm favorite natural and environmental features with youth
- Talk with elders about changes in the environment over the years
- Interview outdoor enthusiasts and related merchants
- Take a guided tour with local nature groups or enthusiasts
- Explore valued environmental features and attributes at a community workshop
- Allow people to respond to a questionnaire (possibly online)
- Facilitate one-on-one interviews
- Conduct discussion groups or focus groups
- Distribute surveys and questionnaires
- Host public workshops
- Lead youth forums
- Take day or night tours of the community
- Participate in site visits
- Host partnership meetings
- Conduct design charrettes
- Organize Web-based chatrooms, etc.
- Attend civic group meetings
- Conduct informal interviews
- Participate in public hearings

Figures 2-172, 2-173, and 2-174. There is no substitute for bringing people together to explore ideas.

Figures 2-175 and 2-176. Community walks are a great way to uncover unique opportunities and share thoughts.

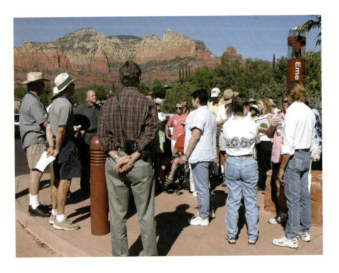

Observation

Ideas for opportunities to make observations include the following:

- Attend historical society meetings, presentations, and other functions
- Go to local plays and other cultural events
- Listen to the outdoor sounds of the local community at different times of the day
- Take walks around town, wandering in the community
- Pay attention to common building materials
- Look for patterns or unique attributes of street, business, and neighborhood names
- Visit key attractions and gathering spots
- Attend local events, including city council meetings
- Review flyers for events for clues about community values
- Visit local businesses
- Pay attention to who is using the local area
- Look in the lobby of hotels for "things to do" and other clues about the community
- Attend local religious services
- Stroll around local art galleries
- Visit the local library
- Observe the natural environment
- Visit a local quarry
- Take hikes or walks in local natural areas
- Watch the outdoor activities that take place
- Pay attention to the smells and scents of the area
- Learn about the wildlife that lives in the local waters, skies, and lands
- Discover the types of plants that grow naturally in the area and are favored in local gardens
- View advertisements and signs posted around town for clues connecting the local area to nature (e.g., "Drains to the Ocean" signs at storm drains)
- Look at the local landscape for clues to industries of yesteryear (e.g., abandoned mining hoists suggest unique geology, rusted farm tractors and fallow fields indicate crops that once flourished, etc.)
- Identify local geologic or geographic landmarks or features (e.g., rock outcropping, hill, view, etc.)
- Learn about local weather patterns and experience weather changes
- Become aware of the geographical context of the town (e.g., at the confluence of two rivers, a port along the seacoast, on Lewis and Clark Trail, etc.)
- View the night skies, sunset, and sunrise

Research

Ideas for researching POAB opportunities include the following:

- Browse local antique shops for historic postcards, photos, and memorabilia
- Research the local library for information on local history and culture, the natural environment, and other community attributes
- Visit the local historical society for archived information on people, activities, events, industries, and other dimensions of place
- Review Sanborn Fire Insurance Maps to identify businesses and other community features that once existed
- Search the archives of local and regional newspapers
- Read the minutes of city council and commission meetings
- Talk with history teachers at local schools
- Review local family genealogies
- Speak to community elders and listen to oral histories
- Visit local cemeteries
- Review outdated community plans and maps
- Talk with architects about the sources for local building materials
- Review weather records and almanacs
- Meet with the local office of tourism or chamber of commerce to learn of existing, as well as past, festivals and special events
- Talk with horticulturalists at a local nursery to learn of local flora, soils, etc.
- Contact local universities, colleges, and cooperative farm extensions to explore a range of natural features
- Review the local general plan, habitat conservation plans, open space plans, or environmental documents to uncover natural resources
- Talk with curators of local and regional museums to learn about the natural environmental features and characteristics of the area, both now and historically
- Talk with governmental agencies, such as the United States Geological Survey, Department of Natural Resources, etc.
- Search the Internet

Figures 2-177 and 2-178. Understanding the community through local eyes is an essential ingredient of Placemaking on a Budget.

CONCLUSION

Connecting people and place is the fundamental goal of placemaking. Through community-based processes that weave together community values (i.e., history, culture, the natural environment, and other community attributes) and community canvases (i.e., architecture, infrastructure, and landscape), communities can lead POAB projects that can be effective conduits for enhancing a sense of local ownership over place. From Enumclaw, Washington, to Harlem, New York, and Hardy, Arkansas, to Sterling, Colorado, communities have created projects that heighten the built environment's meaning and role to people—all because these projects integrate a variety of community values that tap the emotions, pride, and energies of those who live, work, and visit the areas. POAB, through this chapter, provides a meaningful framework that builds upon local history and culture, the natural environment, and community attributes to help communities improve the vitality of the public realm and the connection of people to it.

There are a myriad of different resources available to all communities to implement Placemaking on a Budget.

CHAPTER 3

Placemaking on a Budget Resources

oney is the first resource that comes to mind when thinking about project implementation. But it really is not the most important part of implementing a Placemaking on a Budget project. If you've involved the community and identified a project or projects that resonate with the them, you likely already have many of the resources you'll need to make things happen. Your POAB resources are people, organizations, the private sector, policies and programming, and creative fund-raising. Each different resource group is discussed in this chapter, along with examples of how local resources helped implement POAB projects.

PEOPLE

The theory here is simple—view EVERYONE as a resource. The power of people, as individuals or as a group, should never be underestimated. The "six degrees of separation" phenomenon is definitely one worth applying in POAB implementation planning—everyone knows someone who knows someone who knows someone else who is bound to be a resource to your community project! Individuals can provide ideas, help design projects, build projects, and even maintain projects. By involving people in project development all the way through implementation and maintenance, innovative projects that are owned by the community will result. As described here, you will see that people can be a part of your POAB projects in a variety of different ways.

While specific talents, skills, and expertise clearly are not requirements for getting involved in POAB projects, many people in your community are tremendous resources based upon the unique talents they possess. Find out what skills and talents the members of your community have and create avenues for people to contribute these skills to your POAB projects. As illustrated in many of the public art examples in this PAS Report, visual artists can be an indispensable resource. Artists are important not only for their creativity and talent to create and design projects but also for their ability to help people visualize project ideas through drawings and quick sketches. Of course, "artists" come in many, many forms and may present themselves as sculptors, metalworkers, woodworkers, mason workers, graphic designers, textile designers, or gardeners. You may have architects, landscape architects, planners, engineers, contractors, and construction workers in your community who may be able to help you build and design your POAB projects. Perhaps you will find a gemologist who can identify local stones and gems for use in a creative park bench, a historian who can write interesting local tales to display throughout the town, or even an entomologist who can work with the youth to paint a mural of butterflies from your region. You may find that there are excellent researchers and writers who could be great at finding and writing grant applications. The possibilities are endless! Individuals in your community may or may not be rich with cash, but you will find your communities rich with individual talents and skills.

Figure 3-1. To design their downtown fountain, Azusa, California, was able to tap the talent of a well-known artificial rock creator who just happened to reside in their community.

LOCATING PUBLIC ART IN THE COMMUNITY: AN ARTIST'S PERSPECTIVE

By Donald Fels

Public art is many different things to many different people, but its role in building community and making local character and history visible is often overlooked. Besides functioning as decoration or as monuments, public art can be a way for communities to create links and interpret how and why they settled, developed, and were sustained on the land over the years. Places usually grew because of their proximity to natural resources, water, and transportation corridors. Over time, however, industrial bases change or disappear altogether, man-made and even natural elements become transformed, and what may have been obvious to newcomers a century ago may go completely unnoticed today.

Research is the key to creating meaningful public art about place. Well-researched public art will always be about the place and its people and not about the most recent transformation of the downtown streets. Research involves not only looking in all the usual places—archives, libraries, books—but also talking with older residents, history buffs, and groups of citizens, young and old. Community-oriented artmaking demands time for the research process, which ultimately means that the artist spends real time becoming directly involved with the community itself. This process of involvement serves to ground the artwork in the community and ensures that the public art is about the place as much as it is about the art.

Once themes have been developed through research, the artist can create artwork ideas to show to the public. The quality of the ideas will determine the staying power of the art. The ideas are brought back to the community groups for feedback, which continues the process of involvement. The artist can guide the process so that the community helps winnow the ideas, without the art being designed by committee. Group-created artwork rarely works to anyone's satisfaction. On the other hand, art conceived and created by the artist with a good deal of community input is very often successful. For this process to work well, the artist must be brought in at the project's beginning, and the budget must include sufficient design development time for the artist to work with the community. By its very nature, community-oriented artmaking is not created in a hurry.

In any project there will be more ideas than budget, but if the ideas are based solidly in the place and are creatively interpreted, unexpected resources will often materialize for making them. A community that sees its history and its self-identity validated in artwork will find ways to make ideas happen. Artwork that is true to a place is rare, and citizens enjoy seeing art installed that reflects where and who they are. One important way to make a literal connection to a place is to use local materials and industries in creating the art. Longstanding area manufacturers or material suppliers are usually quite honored to participate in fabricating artwork for their community and often will do a good deal of the work for a reduced cost or even pro bono. Of course, artists should give credit for this assistance and explain the connection of the materials and/or the fabricators to the history of the area. Since a longtime company in the area will have employed generations of local residents, involving these companies also means involving area residents.

Public art based in the local community may not seem as flashy as bringing in a piece of sculpture from a gallery, but ultimately, it will mean more. If artists are involved with the project from the beginning, they can identify places where art can be meaningfully incorporated into the streetscape, sometimes as part of the general construction budget. Therefore, more art gets included at less expense and is distributed throughout the project, which involves the pleasure of discovery for those who will live with it. Making public art in this way is time consuming, takes patience, and is not for every community or every artist. But if there is a match, the process can be wonderfully rewarding for all involved and provide long-lasting pleasure for the community and those who visit there.

As you "tap" the individuals in your community, be sure not to overlook two very important groups of people—senior citizens and youth. Senior citizens have an unsurpassable wealth of knowledge and experience to contribute to community building projects. They have "been there" and "done that" in ways we cannot even begin to imagine. Their past experience and infinite wisdom, combined with a bit more free time that many of our seniors have worked so hard to deserve, make senior citizens important, valuable, and dependable volunteers, leaders, and, most of all, teachers.

Figure 3-3. A dedicated group of senior citizen women plant, weed, and harvest this community garden in Kennewick, Washington.

Figure 3-2. A group of retirees rich with experience and skills in Groveland, California, formed a group called GAINS—Groveland Area Involved Neighbors. Their mission? To implement projects important to the residents of their community.

Youth are also often overlooked in community development and revitalization. Kids offer a level of energy, enthusiasm, and optimism that is difficult to find in our communities. When meaningfully involved, kids are creative, committed, and fun. Youth should be encouraged to get involved as individuals, or with groups of other kids, and should always be invited to participate with adults. Youthful exuberance and ingenuity make the reason to improve the future very clear. (Also see the section in Chapter 2 of the PAS Report, "Seeing the Community Through the Eyes of Your Young People" on page 31).

Figure 3-4. Kids of any age can be a great resource for POAB projects, such as these youngsters in Prescott Valley, Arizona.

Figure 3-5. During a design charrette in Lincoln City, Oregon, young Shelby sat quietly designing a series of elaborate climbing sculptures, complete with internal ladders and water features. She modestly presented her creations at both the design charrette and a city council meeting, and soon, developers were clamoring to build "Shelby's Park."

Figures 3-6 and 3-7. Local scouts are a source of amazing skills and talents, as evidenced in this Calistoga, California, example where a young man constructed this community bulletin board as an Eagle Scout project.

Figures 3-8 and 3-9. This historic water pump in Boalsburg, Pennsylvania, was restored by a young Eagle Scout.

Figure 3-10. Local youth worked with the designers to develop the concept for this festive, interactive climbing sculpture in Cathedral City, California.

People are also a source of ideas, information, and inspiration for POAB projects. The power of bringing people together to explore their community's history, culture, environment, and unique attributes is indescribable. Amazing and creative ideas will emerge when you merely ask people what they think and what they know. As noted in Chapter 2, there are numerous ways to achieve early and meaningful participation, such as holding visioning workshops, organizing community walks, and interviewing residents. In addition to merely contributing their time to develop project ideas, many people will also be willing and anxious to contribute "sweat equity" to the construction and maintenance of projects. People inherently want to do things, and you can capture that energy. Not every project will require a professional skill—there are many simple tasks people can get involved in, especially if supervised and provided with good instruction. It often takes only a strong volunteer spirit, a little time, and a desire to help to be successful at such activities as painting tiles for a mural, cleaning a vacant lot for a new park, laying bricks for a new neighborhood monument, or picking weeds in a new community garden.

Figure 3-11. Even the smallest of children have something to contribute, as shown by this happy little girl in Fort Bragg, California, painting a home for the nonprofit organization Parents and Friends.

A YOUTH-INSPIRED LOGO FOR THE VILLAGE OF TAFT; LINCOLN CITY, OREGON

In Lincoln City, Oregon, senior citizen artists worked side-by-side with middle-school students to develop logos for the Village of Taft. Numerous unique designs came out of the contest, but one logo was selected for the project. The winning design, by 12-year-old Ryan, centered on a crab reminiscent of the area's crabbing history surrounding images of a famous family of local rocks from the Siletz Bay. This logo concept was refined by a local artist and truly began to "brand" the area, including being used on the Village of Taft vision poster, business association jackets, and a beautiful street-spanning arch. This unique logo idea emerged from the creative mind of a twelve-year-old, with no need for an expensive graphic design firm (Figures 3-12 through 3-18).

Figure 3-12 (left). Senior citizen artists coach middle-school students in a logo contest for the Village of Taft.
Figure 3-13 (above). Young Ryan's winning concept included a crab reminiscent of the area's crabbing history surrounding images of a famous family of local rocks from the Siletz Bay.

Figures 3-14 and 3-15. This logo concept was refined by a local artist and truly began to "brand" the area.

Arlon Gilliland/Faye Stroud

Figures 3-16 and 3-17. *The new logo was also used on the Taft business association jackets, as illustrated by this Lincoln City council member.*

Figure 3-18. *This logo concept was also the inspiration for a beautiful street-spanning arch.*

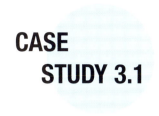

CASE STUDY 3.1

BRINGING UNITY TO THE COMMUNITY, PHOENIX, ARIZONA

By Robert Pikora and Charla McCoy

Freeways are often the most prominent public works in a community. Until recently, however, the design and location of these structures typically considered only safety, efficiency, and cost, and neglected community stability or appearance. Some freeways cut through neighborhoods and isolated schools, parks, shopping, and friends. The structures are often barren of landscaping and use materials, such as concrete or steel, that create dark, neglected, and uninviting spaces beneath them.

Phoenix's Bringing Unity to the Community project, which was originally based on public input during meetings with city departments and the Arizona Department of Transportation, sought to alleviate such problems with six, 40-year-old freeway underpasses. Freeway mitigation projects lessen freeway impacts on residential areas through landscape enhancements, sound walls, trail and pedestrian connections, and land-use policies. The Phoenix Freeway Mitigation program goes beyond normal planning department activities since planners use voter-approved bond funds to write mitigation specific plans (after extensive public outreach and interaction), assign a capital improvement budget, and then implement the projects outlined in the plan.

Residents adjacent to the Maricopa Freeway (Interstate 17) south of downtown Phoenix wanted a safer pedestrian environment, an artistic element that reflected the community's culture, and the involvement of neighborhood kids. The project took place in three phases: overpass improvements, public artwork, and landscape enhancements. Overpass improvements included cleaning and painting the structures, installing bird-netting (to prevent birds from roosting), and replacing a portion of light fixtures. The public artwork phase involved working with two school districts, six elementary schools, 500 students, teachers, parents, principals, neighborhood activists, and six local artists working in three teams. Two basic themes were chosen for the overall project: two base colors, Arizona Sky Blue and Rugged Trail, and "mariposas," the Spanish word for butterflies and the root of the freeway's name. Students further defined specific overpasses with themes based on recycling and protecting the environment, celebrating physical art, music, and literature, local history, and the nearby natural and built environments. The third and final phase, landscaping, replaced and enhanced existing landscaping and ground cover. In keeping with the theme of each underpass, the artists worked with a landscaping consulting firm to extend the artwork beyond the concrete underpasses.

The project took nearly five years from the first public meeting to the celebration of its completion. While the freeway was once just a means to get people from one place to another, the Bringing Unity to Community project demonstrates that underpasses can serve as gateways to Phoenix. The underpasses are no longer a blank canvas for graffiti and vandalism; they are a part of the community, united in color.

Residents were invited to tour the project area with planners and engineers, attend public open houses to review the design concepts by the artists, to participate in the art workshops creating tile pieces, and to participate in the final celebration and bus tour of the project. Another major innovation about the project was its education factor in the elementary schools. In return for students' assistance in the project, Freeway Mitigation and Planning Department staff presented PowerPoint slide shows throughout the school year about urban planning, freeway mitigation and enhancement, and the many functions of Phoenix City Hall. Students and teachers were also involved in expressing their creativity through the art workshops held by the artists in each of the schools. Here, students expanded their literary and visual art skills by participating in ceramic tile workshops, brainstorming ideas through paintings, drawings, and poetry, and presenting their ideas before their peers

and, in some cases, in front of local television cameras. Students learned about recycling and how recycled materials were being used for the project. Student apprentices from the Xicanindio Artes, Incorporated, art program were able to get "hands-on" experience by assisting artist Martin Moreno with the painting of the large-scale murals on the 15th Avenue and 19th Avenue underpasses.

All photos by Bob Pikora

Figures 3-19, 3-20, 3-21, and 3-22: What were once uninviting, negative community features are now celebrated art in these Phoenix neighborhoods.

CELEBRATING THE RETURN OF RAIL: SUMNER, WASHINGTON

By Joseph Schiessl

Since before the incorporation of Sumner, Washington, in 1891, the railroad has served as an important facet of the community's history and growth. The downtown and surrounding residential neighborhoods developed within a 15-minute walk of the railroad depot after the Northern Pacific line arrived in the 1880s. Therefore, when the regional commuter rail service, called "The Sounder," began in September 2000, the entire community, children and adults alike, was involved in welcoming the train back to town.

Citizens had taken an active interest in the creation of a downtown station by participating in design workshops with city staff, Sound Transit representatives, and the design team. As a result, the station's architecture derived its inspiration from a hops kiln, a reflection of the city's agricultural history. The plan received an award from the Washington Chapter of the American Planning Association and the Planning Association of Washington.

Residents were also concerned about incorporating young people and different types of art into the project. In addition to funding from Sumner Promotions Association and Sound Transit, the city and Sumner School District received a $10,000 grant from the Washington State Arts Council to celebrate the opening of the station. Entitled "The Spirit of Sumner," the grant placed an artist-in-residence at four schools in preparation for a community celebration at Sumner High School. A choreographer taught elementary school students a dance. Another elementary school hosted a writer, who helped the students write poetry. Junior-high students wrote and performed an original song about the train with the assistance of a songwriter. A commissioned artist instructed high school students on how to silkscreen street banner designs, which continue to be used throughout the central business district.

With the help of the state grant and the four artists-in-residence, the city and school district were able to engage the youngest members of the community in celebrating an important event in the Sumner's history. Such an effort will likely strengthen the students' ties with their hometown and encourage further local collaboration in the future.

Figure 3-24 (left). *Simple Adopt-a-Block programs like this one in Cincinnati, Ohio, allow individual residents, organizations, or businesses to clean up and maintain neighborhood and city streets.*

Figure 3-25 (right). *Individuals can also take responsibility and care for small public spaces through "adoption" programs. Signs and placards demonstrate an appreciation for the volunteers and their time, as done in this downtown Roseburg, Oregon, public plaza.*

84 | Placemaking on a Budget

Figures 3-26 and 3-27. Leathers & Associates from Ithaca, New York, has built more than 1,600 one-of-a-kind playgrounds using a philosophy that stresses the importance of volunteerism and community. Children actively participate in the design process, and residents donate their labor during construction.

Figure 3-28. This arch over Highway 101 in Willits, California, once proclaimed Reno as "The Biggest Little City in the World." Willits residents donated materials, time, and equipment to refurbish the arch after the city of Reno donated the structure in 1990.

Figure 3-29. Citizens joined forces to create this small park in Old Town Florence, Oregon.

CASE STUDY 3.2

CHANGING OUT AT THE VOLUNTEER CAFÉ, OCEAN BEACH, CALIFORNIA

By Curt Lutz

Ocean Beach is a town that cherishes the status quo. This sentiment is understandable given the community's charming streets, waterfront location, pleasant climate, laid-back lifestyle, and proximity to downtown San Diego. The diverse residents share a desire for simplicity in their lifestyles, homes, and neighborhoods. The question for civic leaders is how to maintain this satisfying sameness.

In light of increasing development pressures and the need for refurbished local infrastructure, the Ocean Beach Community Development Corporation (OBCDC) has found that things *must* change in order to stay the same. The organization, founded in 1994 and led by executive director Curt Lutz, has enhanced streetscapes through planting trees, installing public art, painting commercial properties, and cleaning common areas. In addition, they have assisted local businesses facing competition from chains and founded a domestic violence shelter. At the same time, OBCDC has been involved in the planning process and worked to determine community sentiment through mail surveys.

Obtaining help for all of these initiatives is typically a difficult task. However, OBCDC has made volunteering easier by making the first Saturday of every month a regularly scheduled time for residents to contribute to their community. People meet at a local café that cosponsors the event and alternates from month-to-month. After signing in and having a chance to grab a free coffee and snack, volunteers read through a rundown of tasks for that day. Most projects, which often consist of picking up street or beach trash, weeding, fertilizing, and painting out graffiti, are typically finished within a few hours. OBCDC has also organized larger community and beach cleanups with other local organizations.

OBCDC has also benefited by acquiring a steady and growing group of volunteers. Yet the organization's efforts were made possible thanks to support from different cafés, recognition in the local newspaper, and word of mouth. In the end, the volunteer cafés have served as a simple way for residents to work to make their community a better place and to meet others who share a common commitment to Ocean Beach.

Figure 3-30. The volunteer cafés in Ocean Beach, California, have made volunteering easy.

ORGANIZATIONS

When entering many communities throughout the United States, one is often greeted by a "welcome to" sign with a host of different local organizations proudly displaying their logos. Just as individuals are important POAB resources, these organizations, clubs, and agencies are also a huge resource. There are a plethora of organizations—both formal and informal—available to assist in placemaking efforts. Make it a point to know what organizations exist in your community. Know their missions and their membership, and find ways POAB projects will help them achieve their goals. By doing so, you will discover many new resources!

Service groups and fraternal clubs, such as Rotary, Lions, Optimists/Soroptimists, Masonic Lodge, and Elks,. are a great source of volunteers and sponsorship for POAB projects, as are youth-oriented groups such as Girl Scouts, Boy Scouts, Boys and Girls Clubs, and 4-H. Historical societies, art guilds, theater groups, and other such organizations can also be important resources. Any of these groups can adopt and maintain parks, flower beds, or trees. They can purchase or sponsor benches, water fountains, public art, and signs. They can rally and organize volunteers for participation in community workshops, as well as construction, painting, or repair projects.

Most communities also have numerous informal social clubs and groups organized around specific topics (such as the natural environment, history, books, gardening, and neighborhood safety) or specific activities (such as cards, games, and jogging). These small groups can be equally effective in community building and placemaking projects. Garden clubs can help plant native shrubs and trees; the neighborhood sewing circle can help design and create downtown banners; the bridge club can sponsor a tournament to raise money for materials. There is no limit to the number of organizations in your community, and there is no limit to the ways to involve them in POAB projects.

Figures 3-31 and 3-32. Every community boasts numerous civic clubs and organizations that can become a partner in implementing POAB projects, such as illustrated here in Groveland, California, and Jerome, Arizona.

Figure 3-33. The local Lions Club is responsible for this community bench in Mill Valley, California.

Chapter 3. Placemaking on a Budget Resources 87

Figures 3-34, 3-35, and 3-36. "Legacy of Beauty" tiles highlight the names of individuals and groups that have sponsored planters and other amenities in the San Gabriel, California, Mission District.

Figure 3-37. A dedicated garden club planted and continues to maintain these community flowers in Groveland, California.

88 Placemaking on a Budget

Figure 3-40. This lovely park was sponsored by and named for the local Rotary Club of Temecula, California.

Figures 3-38 and 3-39. Many community amenities are made possible through the generous contributions of local organizations, clubs, and groups, such as this bench in State College, Pennsylvania, and this fountain in Downtown Pleasanton, California.

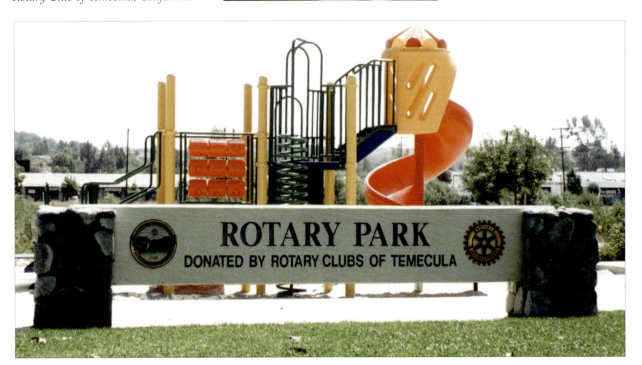

STRONG PARTNERSHIPS

Forging partnerships with public agencies is yet another way to leverage organizational power. A good example of this type of partnership is the Oregon Coast Weather Center in Lincoln City, Oregon, presented in Chapter 2. The simple idea of a rain gauge was unexpectedly and wildly embraced by the community members and ultimately snowballed into an idea for a full-fledged weather and tsunami center by the end of the meeting. A local artist gave even more life to the idea by preparing a concept sketch of the finished center. Through the hard work and excitement of these community supporters, a variety of different partners were attracted to help work on making the idea a reality, including national, state, regional, and local entities. Among the national partners are the U.S. Department of Commerce, the Weather Channel, the National Oceanic and Atmospheric Association (NOAA), the National Weather Service, as well as federal legislators. State partners included Portland State University, Oregon State University, Oregon Emergency Management, Oregon State Tourism Department, Oregon State Department of Agriculture, Oregon Economic and Community Development Department, and members of the Oregon House of Representatives and Senate. In addition, the partnership also included many local and regional partners, such as the Oregon Museum of Science and Industry, Oregon Coast Aquarium, television, radio, and newspapers, as well as a large number of individual and corporatesponsors. These partnerships are an integral part of the ultimate implementation of the Oregon Coast Weather Center (Figures 3-41 through 3-45).

If there are universities, community colleges, trade schools, or other specialty schools (e.g., music, art, culinary) in your region, look for unique ways to get them involved. Institutions of higher education

Figures 3-41 and 3-42.
Community leaders and other partners working to bring the Oregon Coast Weather Center to life have developed two possible logos.

Logos by Lincoln City Urban Renewal Agency

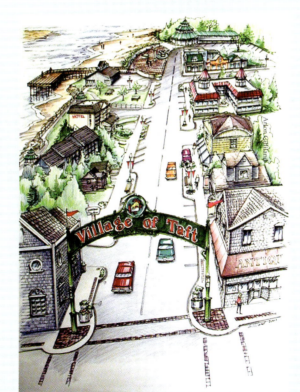

Figure 3-43.
A local artist brings the weather center idea alive through his artistic interpretation.

STRONG PARTNERSHIPS *(continued)*

often have many unique resources at their disposal and can play key roles in your POAB efforts, not the least of which is a pool of talented and enthusiastic students and instructors. Instructors are always looking for real-life projects for their students and generally have a commitment to support the communities in which they are located.

Your community is unique and distinct so it follows that the set of organizations you uncover will be different than those found in any other place in the country. Likewise, the ways in which you involve them in POAB projects will also vary. And remember, encourage the involvement of local organizations early in the process—don't wait until the last minute and expect them to be as excited about your project as you and your committee are!

Figures 3-45 and 3-46. Planning students, staff, and faculty, such as those at the University of California at Irvine and the University of Oregon, work with local communities on a variety of projects. They benefit both communities looking for expertise and students looking for experience.

ROSEBURG'S DOWNTOWN ARCHES: ROSEBURG, OREGON

In January 1999, Roseburg, Oregon, adopted a downtown master plan for its Roseburg Town Center. Among other important implementation goals, the Roseburg community envisioned the construction of two gateway arches signaling arrival into downtown. A host of volunteers worked for three years to realize a preferred design and to identify and align local community resources to both fabricate and install the gateway arches at a minimal cost. In January 2002, the first archway was installed after a collaborative and largely volunteer effort by the Roseburg Town Center Board and the Umpqua Valley Home Builders Association, as well as an architect, an engineer, and a construction company from the community. The second archway was constructed later that year, again tapping the volunteer and in-kind resources within the Roseburg community. Through its persistence and focus, the Roseburg community achieved its goal to have special entries into its town center that welcomed visitors and residents alike.

Figures 3-47 and 3-48. The Roseburg archway was installed after a collaborative and largely volunteer effort by the Roseburg Town Center Board, the Umpqua Valley Home Builders Association, as well as an architect, an engineer, and a construction company from the community.

FORT BRAGG'S ONE-OF-A-KIND BENCHES, FORT BRAGG, CALIFORNIA

The community members of Fort Bragg, California, adjacent to the beautiful Redwood Forest, wanted downtown benches that enhanced the unique character of this beach community. Recognizing the numerous rare resources at its disposal, Fort Bragg brainstormed with leaders from the Fine Woodworkers Association, the College of the Redwoods, Georgia Pacific, and Adirondack Designs (a local company in which people with mental and physical disabilities build outdoor wood furniture). The resulting strategy was a bench design competition sponsored by the Fine Woodworkers. Lumber was donated by Georgia Pacific, and workers from Adirondack Designs and students of the College of the Redwoods were going to be invited to build the various benches.

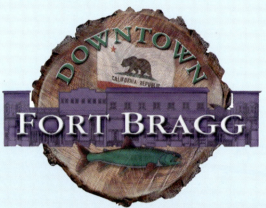

Figure 3-49. To create unique downtown benches, the City of Fort Bragg capitalized on its connection to the Redwood Forest, the Fine Woodworkers Association, and the College of the Redwoods, as well as the private resources of Georgia Pacific Lumber Company and Adirondack Designs.

RBF Consulting's Urban Design Studio/Faye Stroud

Figures 3-50 and 3-51. Adirondack Designs, supported by a local nonprofit organization, employs individuals with developmental disabilities to build wonderful wood furniture that is sold all over the country.

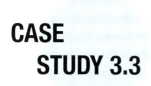

CASE STUDY 3.3

NAPPANEE SENIORS RETURN TO SCHOOL: NAPPANEE, INDIANA

By Larry Andrews

When the Nappanee Boys and Girls Club decided to lease the vacant Central School building, the organization knew that it might have bitten off more than it could chew. The chapter was new and the lease payments would be a significant drain on the organization's budget. Despite renting parts of the building to the Nappanee Chamber of Commerce, the city's Redevelopment Commission, a dance studio, and a local church group, club staff realized that they needed to explore other options in order to ease their financial crunch.

The Boys and Girls Club found willing partners in the city, the Redevelopment Commission, the Chamber of Commerce, the Family Christian Development Center, Justus Property Management, and Brown & Brown Construction. Together, they proposed the construction of 22 senior housing units in and around the building. The project provided a number of benefits, including:

(1) the city's communitywide housing study had just identified the need for additional affordable senior housing and had grant funds to support such a venture;

(2) the school's close proximity to downtown would enable seniors to access services and patronize local merchants; and

(3) the seniors could use the club's gym, game room, and computers during school hours and provide mentoring for the children after school.

Strong local support allowed the partners to raise the $2.4 million needed to refurbish the building, including grants from the federal HOME program, the Indiana Department of Commerce and Housing Finance Authority, and a local bank.

The revitalization has been a gratifying experience for the numerous residents that attended elementary school at the Central School building. However, the project held more than just emotional benefits. Different members of Nappanee's public and private sector all found something compelling and worthwhile about supporting a venture that helped the city's youth, seniors, and downtown.

Figure 3-52. A revitalized Central School Building in Nappanee, Indiana.

PRIVATE SECTOR

In the same manner that local civic, not-for-profit, and social organizations can get involved in placemaking efforts, so too can the private sector. Local merchants, property owners, major employers, and even the local media can play a major role in making great things happen in your community. These organizations are able to donate materials, labor, land, and the use of storefronts, windows, doors, and building walls, as well as to sponsor a variety of community amenities. The private sector is often eager to get involved in community building projects because these types of endeavors generally have the potential to enhance identification, marketing, and economic vitality.

Figure 3-53. Inexpensive planter pots throughout downtown Brookings, Oregon, are sponsored and maintained by a local business group.

Figure 3-54. Community-minded businesses can donate space for local bulletin boards or community announcements, as evidenced in Noah's Bagels in Corvallis, Oregon.

Figure 3-55. Business-sponsored trash receptacles in downtown Corvallis, Oregon, provide a necessary public amenity, while at the same time advertise the business itself.

Figure 3-56. A window sign in Kennewick, Washington, celebrates the successful road improvements funded by local downtown businesses.

Chapter 3. Placemaking on a Budget Resources 95

Figure 3-57. *The simple act of placing a bowl of water on the sidewalk, as done by this Laguna Beach, California, business owner, encourages pet owners to linger and enjoy the downtown.*

Figure 3-59. A downtown clock is installed by a local jewelry business in Mount Healthy, Ohio.

Figure 3-58. This bench in Laguna Beach, California, sponsored by a local inn, celebrates the life of a well-loved resident.

Figures 3-60 and 3-61. Local merchants come together to fund these attractive hanging flowers in downtown Toledo, Oregon.

96 Placemaking on a Budget

Figure 3-62. Various businesses sponsor charming sidewalk plaques along San Francisco's Fisherman's Wharf.

Figure 3-63. Local businesses are responsible for the lush planting in this New Orleans park.

Figures 3-64 and 3-65. Merchants in downtown State College, Pennsylvania, joined forces to sponsor a colorful mural on a blank building wall.

Figure 3-66. The base of this piece of public art along the New Orleans waterfront identifies the many private sponsors that helped to make it possible.

Your local media can also be an excellent POAB implementation resource. Your community cable and radio stations, local newspapers, and other community publications can encourage people to get involved in a project by sharing the message of community building. They can promote and cover POAB projects and stories, and they can also get involved on a more personal level. Individual members of the media generally have a pulse on community interests and know about unique aspects of a town or neighborhood that can contribute greatly to placemaking efforts. Viewing and involving the local media as your partner in the process can yield great things.

Figure 3-67. Tapping the resource of your local media personalities and outlets, as occurs regularly in Prescott Valley, Arizona, should not be overlooked.

Figure 3-68. In Lincoln City, Oregon, the local newspaper became so involved in the revitalization efforts that they established a project Web site for the community on their own accord.

CASE STUDY 3.4

REALIZING THE POWER OF PARTNERSHIPS IN ST. ANDREWS, PANAMA CITY, FLORIDA

By Nancy Wengel and Allara Mills Gutcher

During the mid-twentieth century, the historic St. Andrews neighborhood was a lively village with a healthy economy based on tourism and charter fishing. The area's prosperity changed in the late 1970s and early 1980s when the main highway through the neighborhood was rerouted north of St. Andrews, and tourist and boat traffic shifted to other locations along the Gulf of Mexico. The neighborhood became a ghost town.

Efforts at revitalizing the community began in earnest in the early 1990s when residents successfully challenged a proposed waterfront mall and condominium project. Instead, the land became a park that is now home to numerous community celebrations. The effort to create the park was sponsored by the newly created St. Andrews Waterfront Partnership, a not-for-profit organization formed by business owners and residents and endorsed by the city commission. Over the last decade, the city and partnership have overseen the creation of a new waterfront boardwalk, renovation of the marina, and completion of many other projects, all of which have been important in reviving the local economy.

Strong public and private support has been critical to St. Andrews's success. Since 1994, there has been roughly $15 million of government and private investment in the area. Residents have donated countless hours of their time working on different projects. The city's Community Redevelopment Agency has helped pay for "bricks and mortar expenses" while the partnership's additional fund-raising supports important undertakings. The salary of the full-time project director is split between city and state grant funding.

The partnership's considerable financial backing is due in large part to building and maintaining personal relationships. The area's city commissioner has a permanent seat on the board. The project director has lived in St. Andrews for 20 years and has a strong network of contacts. Perhaps most importantly, though, the partnership has focused on communicating with residents, including constructing an information kiosk and publishing a monthly newsletter with a circulation of 200 residents.

Figure 3-69. Strong partnerships were key to the revitalization of the St. Andrews neighborhood in Panama City, Florida.

CASE STUDY 3.5

MIRACLE ON 4TH STREET PARK, LONG BEACH, CALIFORNIA

By Angie Avery

Leadership Long Beach is an organization dedicated to developing community leaders by getting different groups of professionals involved in important city projects. The Class of 2000 wanted to create a project that would dramatically improve a neighborhood, have a lasting impact, and improve the lives of children. Creating a mini park could accomplish these objectives but finding a location, either city owned or available for lease, would be extremely difficult.

At the eleventh hour, Kim and Daryl Rouse, owners of a 6,000-square-foot lot near the corner of 4th Street and Walnut Avenue, came to the project's rescue. The Rouses, who also owned the adjacent laundromat, determined that the empty lot was not suitable for building. They also felt that the neighborhood children sorely needed a place to play and that the alley behind their property provided a poor substitute. The need for green space and community pride in this densely populated neighborhood was undeniable. Leadership Long Beach, along with Councilman Dan Baker's office, several city officials, the Long Beach Job Corps, and the Conservation Corps of Long Beach, soon started work with the Rouses and the community.

Class-of-2000 participants pulled together potential design elements for the park, including a place where young children could climb on play equipment and where their parents could sit and watch from a shady spot. They also envisioned a magnificent mural on the side of the laundromat. After canvassing the neighborhood with flyers, the team then led two community meetings. They presented three proposed park layouts at the first meeting and listened to resident concerns. Specifically, some residents of the neighboring condominium complex were worried about noise, and many wanted to keep the park free from drugs and gangs. The second meeting was held two weeks later to share the final design proposal, which was well received. Through these meetings, neighbors became acquainted with one another and united in support of the plan to beautify the neighborhood.

The collaborators began developing a budget in order to determine how much funding was needed. The Long Beach Parks, Recreation and Marine Department, the Long Beach Community Development Department, and the Public Corporation for the Arts contributed to the effort. Team members created a fund-raising packet to solicit donations, which were held in trust by Partners of Parks. They eventually received more than $25,000 in donations, which was enough money to build the park. After negotiating a lease, the concept was approved by the city council.

Since Long Beach parks have distinct personalities, the project team wanted to generate community investment in the park by creating a distinct name. After considering potential park name entries from a local fifth-grade class, the park committee chose student Jimmy Scotto's submission: "Miracle on 4th Street Park." The name symbolized the process of creating the park and what it likely represents to the residents of the community.

Groundbreaking and construction of the park began in late spring 2000 with the unveiling of a sign painted by a mural artist. Councilman Baker's office arranged for many of the project participants to receive proclamations from the city council and mayor. In addition, the project received significant media coverage. When the grand opening occurred in the fall, the community was able to celebrate both the opening of a new park in Long Beach, and, perhaps equally as significant, the creation of a new spirit in the neighborhood near 4th and Walnut. It is a park designed by members of the community and named by neighborhood children. Miracle on 4th Street Park has brought people together, created an identity for this neighborhood, and allowed children a place to soar as high as their imaginations will take them.

Figures 3-70, 3-71, and 3-72. Designed by members of the community, Miracle on 4th Street Park is a great example of collaboration and teamwork.

POLICIES AND PROGRAMMING

Tools that don't quickly come to mind when trying to strengthen a sense of place are those related to policies and programming. Zoning, design guidelines, development incentives, and the permitting process, when thoughtfully developed and administered, can help make place "happen." Instead of making it difficult to create vibrant, mixed-use projects or impossible to close off a street for a block party, create incentives and build processes that encourage these types of activities. Program your otherwise dead or dying spaces with music, kids' birthday parties, art displays, and theater. Be specific about what you want to happen in your community and put incentives and policies in place that allow and encourage people to make it happen.

Figures 3-73 and 3-74. Permitting outdoor display of merchandise on sidewalks can inject color and interest along commercial storefronts, as illustrated in this fruit display in Albany, California.

Figures 3-75 and 3-76. Programming public spaces with farmers markets and similar types of activities goes a long way toward creating vitality, such as these in Fort Bragg, California (top), and Kansas City, Missouri (right).

Figure 3-77.
Permitting street vendors, such as flower carts like this one in Coronado, California, is an easy way to enliven otherwise dull pedestrian environments.

Figures 3-78 and 3-79.
Allowing outdoor vending carts provides built-in activity to these outdoor spaces in Denver and New Orleans.

Figures 3-80, 3-81, and 3-82. Spaces that allow outdoor musicians, street performers, and other such activities can enliven the environment as happens along Berkeley's Fourth Street and New Orlean's French Quarter.

Figure 3-83. Outdoor displays of art and other wares can increase the economic and social vitality of a place, as seen throughout the French Quarter in New Orleans.

Figure 3-84. Policies that encourage sidewalk dining are simple placemaking tools. In this case in Mountain View, California, where sidewalk space is tight, the city allows a business to use an on-street parking space for outdoor dining.

Figure 3-85. *Establishing policies and guidelines that encourage creative business signs, like this one in Milwaukee, Wisconsin, can do much to personalize and add unique elements to commercial districts.*

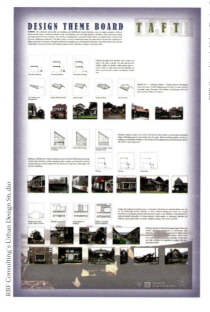

Figures 3-86 and 3-87. *Design guidelines can help to enhance a sense of place but need not be a voluminous and expensive document. As illustrated in Lincoln City and Medford, Oregon, a poster with simple sketches, brief text, and local photos can help establish good design precedent.*

Figure 3-88. *Planning commissioners and interested residents were asked to submit photos of desired architectural design in historic downtown San Juan Bautista, California. The images were ranked in a community meeting and a collage of the top images were used to help guide new development.*

Figure 3-89. *Allowing for simple and creative touches, such as Old Town Albuquerque's rickshaw that transports people from one locale to another, helps to ease traffic congestion while also creating a unique community attraction.*

CREATIVE FUNDRAISING

Ideally, you will have so much donated material, talent, labor, and skill that you won't need to raise cash or obtain grant funding. However, depending on the scale of your project, you may need some money to make it happen. If you need to raise money, be sure to use it as an opportunity to strengthen community and enhance a sense of place. Be creative, be unique, make it fun, and be true to your community identity.

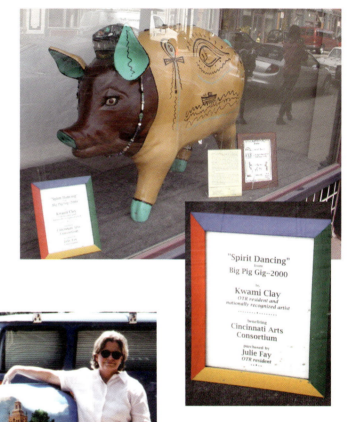

Figures 3-90, 3-91, 3-92, 3-93, and 3-94. Public art projects, such as the Painted Ponies in Albuquerque; the Pigs in Cincinnati; and the Cows on Parade in Kansas City, New York, and Chicago, help a community raise funds. Such endeavors are not only moneymakers, they also enrich communities with unique public art features that attract visitors and residents alike.

Figure 3-95 and 3-96. The Fisherman's Memorial plaza along the Oregon coastline was made possible through many sponsors who are identified in the bricks that outline the modest space.

Figure 3-97. To develop a needed restroom facility in California's historic downtown Placerville, the community organized a unique and fun fund-raising effort. The group sold toilet paper in "I Pottied in Placerville" packaging. Volunteer labor and donated materials were also essential components of this creative project.

Figures 3-98 and 3-99. This plaza in Chattanooga, Tennessee, was constructed through the generosity of numerous individuals who sponsored bricks.

Figure 3-100. Selling bricks, stones, or pavers is an excellent way to both raise funds and directly involve the community in local projects.

Figure 3-101. A creative way to raise money and to reuse old parking meters is found on the sidewalks of downtown Sacramento. This parking meter attracts attention through its unexpected location and encourages passers-by to drop in spare coins to raise funds for the homeless in this case.

Figure 3-102. Each winter, Vienna, Austria, transforms its Town Hall windows into an advent calendar to celebrate the season and to fund-raise! Every day, a window cover is lifted to reveal artwork that will later be purchased by a private entity to raise money for charitable purposes.

Figures 3-103 and 3-104. Kid Town, a park in Brookings, Oregon, was made possible through a truly collective community effort. Each board used to construct the castle-like play equipment is engraved with the name of individuals, families, or groups who donated labor and/or funds.

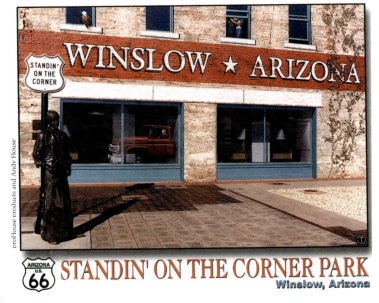

Figure 3-105. The City of Seattle's Small Sparks program provides grants of up to $250 for residents to coordinate small neighborhood events with the aim of creating a stronger community. Small Sparks' coaches help grant recipients organize projects in order to take advantage of existing neighborhood resources.

Figure 3-106. Inspired by the lyric, "Well, I'm standin' on a corner in Winslow, Arizona," from The Eagles' hit song, "Take It Easy," Winslow residents purchased paving bricks to raise funds for a sculpture and mural. The Standin' on the Corner park has become a popular tourist attraction, helped revitalize downtown Winslow, and has been the center of an annual festival.

Figures 3-107 and 3-108. The Tahoe City (California) Beautification Project, an initiative by the Placer County Redevelopment Agency, sought to restore the city's commercial district through new benches, lighting, landscaping, and other items. The agency offered potential donors a "menu" of amenities from which to contribute, ranging from a $25 bulb patch to sidewalk lights.

Figure 3-109. The Heritage Square Trust in Flagstaff, Arizona, produced this flyer to solicit donations of bricks, plaques, and benches in order to renovate the square, billed as the community's "outdoor living room." The organization has successfully completed its original plans but sells bricks in order to fund continued construction, landscaping, and maintenance.

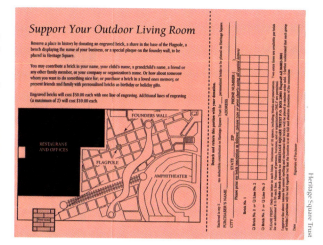

Figures 3-110 and 3-111. During the general plan update process in the town of Prescott Valley, Arizona, the community advisory committee used a plastic piggy bank to raise money. The committee asked members to contribute their spare change at each meeting to raise money to build a community-based project at the end of the process (they also asked the consultant team to pay a quarter each time they used the word "city" instead of "town"!).

Figure 3-112. A simple sign encourages participation in the Millennial Brick Project, helping to fund the library improvements in Signal Hill, California.

Figure 3-113. The contributions of many individuals were responsible for the centennial sculpture in State College, Pennsylvania.

CASE STUDY 3.6

RESTORING THE TOWN COMMON ONE BRICK AT A TIME, GOFFSTOWN, NEW HAMPSHIRE

By Robbie Grady

Like many New England communities, Goffstown has, at its heart, a lively common that serves as host to local celebrations and honors past war dead with a stirring monument. Yet back in 1999, the common was largely unused, strewn with litter, and home to a statue with a broken nose. Civic groups and individuals hesitated to use the park because there was no electricity or running water.

Fresh from another successful parks project, the Village Business Association, the Goffstown Rotary Club, and Goffstown Main Street were among the first organizations to see the potential in the declining property. A local landscape architect created a conceptual plan to revitalize the common, which consisted of installing fountains, lights, brick pathways, and plantings. Civic leaders had a plan, but since the town government lacked funds for the project, they faced a significant obstacle to implementation. They employed a number of fund-raising strategies. Main Street merchants sold engraved bricks and granite pavers, and local businesses provided in-kind donations. Eventually, volunteers laid 19,000 bricks, many of which were engraved, in the common. Browsing through the bricks' messages, which included two marriage proposals, became a popular local activity. The town government and local businesses contributed labor and materials towards excavation, grading, plumbing, construction, lighting, and landscaping. A team of coordinators recruited a cross section of the community, including school children, college students, the *Goffstown News* staff, civic groups, families, and senior citizens, to help with the project. Eventually, organizers estimated that the value of in-kind and cash donations totaled approximately $200,000.

The official opening of the common in October 1999 was marked with music, food, multiple events, and speeches. Since that time, concerts, heritage and holiday festivals, countless picnics, and the Giant Pumpkin Weigh-off and Regatta Festival have been held at the park. The project won the New Hampshire Main Street Center's 1999 Best Public Improvement Project and Best Private/Public Partnership awards. The town has certainly not forgotten the lessons of the park's revitalization. A different group of citizens employed the same model of volunteerism and in-kind donations to renovate a public beach along an unattractive lakefront. This formula has illustrated the community's willingness to come together and lend a hand in order to make Goffstown a more livable place.

Figures 3-114 and 3-115. The Goffstown, New Hampshire, town common restoration illustrates the community's willingness to come together and lend a hand.

CASE STUDY 3.7

CHARLIE, THE "CAN MAN," GROVELAND AND BIG OAK FLATS, CALIFORNIA

Groveland and Big Oak Flats are small Sierra Nevada communities near Yosemite National Park. Volunteerism is alive and well in both communities, an important attribute that has helped address various needs throughout history. Over a decade ago, a group of determined residents set out to find a way to build a much needed and desired museum and library—without the use of public money. The Southern Tuolumne County Historical Society led a broad-based community coalition to raise the funds needed to realize the long-lived dream of the Groveland Yosemite Gateway Museum.

Figure 3-116. The Groveland Yosemite Gateway Museum was funded partly by volunteerism on the part of determined residents.

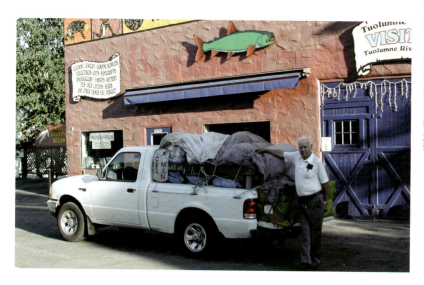

Figures 3-117 and 3-118. Charlie "Can Man" Heath raised a good portion of the money for the museum project by converting oil drums into aluminum can collection sites.

One community member, Charlie "Can Man" Heath, raised more than $45,000 toward the $600,000 project by picking up and recycling aluminum cans over a 10-year period. How and why did Charlie do this? During his retirement years, Charlie was faced with some health challenges that required him to maintain a more active lifestyle. In an effort to do his part to help make the museum and library dream come true, and to improve his health, Charlie reached back to his younger days when he worked in the oil fields in Bakersfield. Charlie collected numerous oil drums and transformed them into aluminum can collection sites located throughout Groveland and Big Oak Flats.

Throughout each week for more than a decade, and continuing today, Charlie would visit each oil drum to collect aluminum cans deposited by locals and visitors—often times, Charlie would walk to collection sites for exercise! Over the course of his aluminum can collections, Charlie wore out several pick-up trucks hauling 800–1,200 pounds of cans and bottles to recycling centers in Modesto. Today, as a result of Charlie's efforts and the efforts of other Groveland and Big Oak Flats residents, the communities now have their long-awaited Groveland Yosemite Gateway Museum. With the success of the library and museum behind them, the community—including Charlie—has raised more than $20,000 toward the development of a skateboard park for area youth!

CONCLUSION

After reading this chapter, your mind should be overflowing with many resources potentially at your disposal. Whether it is the neighborhood garden club, the local cable station, a high school art class, a nearby metal foundry, a new creative sign program, or even your own special variety of "Charlie the Can Man," there is no end to the people and tools that can and should be involved in your POAB efforts. Know your community well and be open to the many ideas and various types of assistance that comes from involving local residents, organizations, and the private sector early in the process. Welcome the use of local policy, programs, and creative fund-raising schemes to implement your placemaking projects. For additional help, see the Chapter 3 Toolkit in Appendix A of this report.

Communities that are most successful in realizing their visions are those that organize and plan for implementation—identifying who, what, when, where, why, how, and how much for each step of a placemaking project.

CHAPTER 4

Implementation

eveloping project ideas is considered by many of us as the most straightforward and, perhaps, the most fun-filled dimension of placemaking. Realizing project ideas—that is, implementing the steps needed to see them become built projects—is often viewed as challenging and, sometimes, overwhelming. The purpose of this chapter is to present considerations for organizing and presenting implementation efforts that simplify your efforts to realize project ideas and optimize your community's ability to bring to life their POAB projects.

Placemaking projects are most likely to be built when implementation is considered during the project identification and selection process. When an idea surfaces for a placemaking project, opportunities should also be explored for resources that could help nurture the idea into a built project (e.g., Does anyone have thoughts on who may help us design and construct this project? or What civic groups do you think may want to get involved in this effort?). Too often, meaningful ideas for placemaking projects will surface only to be discounted by a vocal few due to their inability to think creatively or their orientation towards identifying implementation obstacles rather than implementation possibilities (e.g., We'll never be able to do that—we don't have the money! or City Hall will not allow us to do this.).

POAB is premised on an implementation philosophy very different than this latter perspective. If a community has the capacity to define and carefully articulate the placemaking projects it wants (i.e., the "ends"), and these projects are soundly rooted in community values, it too has the capacity to identify the resources and implement the steps needed to realize the ideas (i.e., the "means"). This chapter, then, presents a framework for helping communities heighten their effectiveness at realizing POAB projects.

READY-AIM-FIRE

Placemaking relies upon the need to first focus on defining specific and achievable projects (i.e., ends) and then to systematically (and in a coordinated fashion) put in place the implementation steps (i.e., means) needed to realize the identified projects. When a placemaking project is identified, implementation of a POAB project (i.e., means) relies upon a methodology embodied in the concept of Ready-Aim-Fire (Figure 4-1).

- READY: Is the "community" organized, engaged, and informed about the project?
- If "Yes," then it is READY and can proceed to AIM. If "No," continue working toward READY.
- AIM: Have issues and ideas been raised and consensus reached on desired actions?
- If "Yes," then the community has its AIM and can proceed to FIRE. If "No," continue working toward AIM.
- FIRE: Are the resources aligned, secured, and ready to implement?
- If "Yes," then initiate project implementation by utilizing your Project Worksheet or a Project Action Plan. If "No," continue working until confident you are ready to FIRE.

Figure 4-1. Ready-Aim-Fire provides a tried-and-tested process for POAB projects.

CREATE ORDER OUT OF CHAOS

Many independent actions and resources need to come together in a focused direction to realize POAB projects. "Project management" is the official term applied to the discipline of bringing these pieces together to a fruitful end. Many communities rely upon software programs and consultants to manage placemaking projects; however, through a thorough understanding of the following seven key questions, communities can manage most if not all of the implementation of POAB projects on their own:

- **What** is the project and what are the individual components of the project?

- **Where** will the project be located and/or where is the project's area of influence?

- **Why** is the project desired or needed?

- **When** should the project most likely be realized (e.g., Is it a short- or long-term project)?

- **Who** will lead the project and who will serve on the team to help implement?

- **How much** will the project cost to implement and maintain? How much of the cost of the project can be reduced through in-kind or donated resources?

- **How** does the project relate to other planned or existing projects and how will the project be funded or otherwise made possible (including grant writing, volunteerism, permitting, in-kind services, etc.)?

In large measure, the first four questions—what, where, why, and when—were explored in Chapter 2 through the identification of placemaking projects. Through the discussion on resources for placemaking projects, as presented in Chapter 3, answers to the last three implementation questions—who, how much, and how—were revealed. Collectively, the answers to these seven questions, when understood for a placemaking project, will optimize a community's ability to implement.

ORGANIZATION TOOLS FOR IMPLEMENTATION EFFECTIVENESS

Organizing these answers in a manner understandable to all who are or will be involved in the process of implementing a POAB project is a very important next step to realizing success. As a general rule, one of the following two formats may be useful to your community when implementing a POAB project: A Project Worksheet or a Project Action Plan (Figure 4-2).

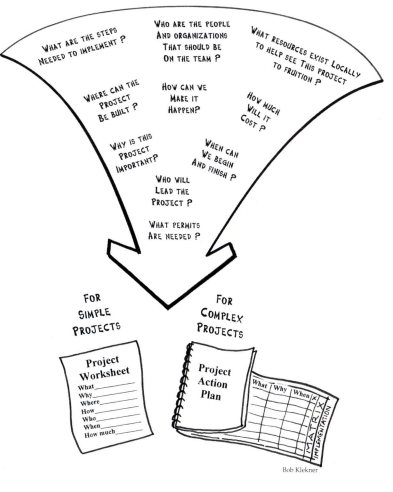

Figure 4-2. The success of implementing POAB projects relies in part on asking many questions and organizing the answers in an orderly and action-oriented manner.

Bob Klekner

Project Worksheet

For simple projects involving few partnerships, a very short timeframe, or a very limited number of implementation steps, a project worksheet may benefit your community when planning your efforts to realize an envisioned POAB project. As Figure 4-3 illustrates, a project worksheet can be prepared with answers to each of the above-listed seven questions presented on a single page. (Folders can also be maintained as supplements to a project worksheet for pictures, maps, pamphlets, and other inspiring materials that will help with your implementation efforts.)

As an example of how a project worksheet may be used for a POAB project, let us consider a community group's vision to transform a nondescript utility cabinet along a sidewalk into an attractive and visually engaging amenity by painting a mural onto it. It is anticipated that in-kind services, donated materials, and volunteer labor will be involved in achieving this vision. Approval for this project will be needed from the local electric company, as well as the city's public works department. To develop a design, the community group will tap a historian from the museum (who will share stories of the community with school children), children from a junior high art class (who will develop design concepts for the mural), and the talents of a local artist (who will interpret the children's concepts and paint the mural onto the utility cabinet). The supplies needed for this project will be sought from local hardware and art supply stores. It is expected to take two weeks to receive approval for the project, another two weeks to work with the students and collect the needed supplies, and a weekend to paint the mural.

A project worksheet for this project may be presented as follows:

- **What:** Painted mural on a utility cabinet depicting dimensions of the community's history; utility cabinet will need to be cleaned prior to painting.

- **Where:** The utility cabinet is located at the corner of Main Street and Market Avenue, the center of the community.

- **Why:** The utility cabinet is an eyesore, painted green with graffiti and stickers.

- **When:** The project will take a total of five weeks, with promotion occurring concurrently with approval, mural concept development, and painting.

- **Who:** The community group will lead the effort; team members will include: local artist; local historian; elementary school principal, art teacher, and art students; hardware store owner; art supply store manager; public works director; electric utility company liaison; local ceramics shop; others.

- **How much:** The project will be achieved through in-kind services, donated materials, and volunteer labor; project maintenance will be the responsibility of the community group.

- **How:** The mural project will be achieved through in-kind services, donated materials, and volunteer labor; funding for ongoing maintenance of the project will be raised through donations made by customers of three popular shops near the utility cabinet (a local ceramic shop has volunteered to make miniature utility cabinet "piggy banks" that will be placed near the cash registers of the three shops); promotion of the project will occur through press releases issued by the community group to the local cable access channel, the two local newspapers, and the one local AM radio station, as well as through the posting of flyers around town.

PLACEMAKING ON A BUDGET **Project Worksheet**

WHAT? _____

WHERE? _____

WHY? _____

WHEN? _____

WHO? _____

HOW MUCH? _____

HOW? _____

Faye Stroud

Figure 4-3. Project Worksheets provide a framework for simple POAB projects.

Project Action Plan

For complex projects that entail many team members, significant fund-raising efforts, a phased schedule for completion, or many implementation steps, a more detailed project action plan may be appropriate. A project action plan is intended to be a brief document that breaks down larger projects or a community vision for an area into smaller pieces that become more manageable by a community considering implementation. A project action plan may be organized into several sections that articulate the various dimensions of a POAB project; one critical element of all project action plans should be an implementation matrix that summarizes responses to the seven questions for each step of the project. For instance, a project action plan may be organized as follows:

- **The Vision for the POAB Project for Your Community:** This section answers **what** the projects are, **why** they are important, and **where** they may occur. (Note: Your community would rephrase this section heading to identify your specific placemaking project or community name.)

The vision may be for revitalizing the entire neighborhood (i.e., **where**) in which the utility cabinet, presented in the project worksheet example above, is located. The neighborhood's revitalization strategy includes numerous POAB

KEEPING MOTIVATED THROUGH A PLACEMAKING PROCESS

By Kurt Olsen

Leading the process to realize placemaking, while certainly worthwhile, is not an easy task. To establish a foundation for placemaking, a process should begin with energy, enthusiasm, and several initial steps:

- Develop a vision of what you want to become
- Establish a plan around core values
- Create a strategy for how you intend to get there
- Determine the roles of those who can make it happen.

Between planning for a placemaking project and implementing it, reality sets in as details are addressed. These details are often draining to the energy developed during the visioning process. The success of a great placemaking project is contingent on keeping your enthusiasm—despite the details—and the vision alive. So what are the secrets to maintaining excitement and motivation?

Figure 4-4. Sharing and celebrating placemaking successes with others is an energizing source of motivation and community building, as occurs regularly in Lincoln City, Oregon.

Avoid looking at a vision plan as one grand project. Break the plan down into individual projects and break those projects down into attainable steps. Each step is a completed goal and a success to build on. These individual steps maintain the momentum to achieve the overall plan. It is important to keep the community involved and remind them that the vision is critical—no matter what challenges or obstacles surface.

A few additional ways that can serve to keep you on track, energized, and motivated include the following:

- Solving a problem or working through a glitch—no matter how small or large, overcoming a challenge is very motivating
- Charting progress and keeping track of successes—keeping track of progress can provide great satisfaction
- Holding ribbon cuttings and dedication celebrations for each project—be sure to include elected officials and invite a local grade school class
- Including the community in celebrating placemaking projects—popular techniques include staging a community photo or having a community picnic
- Creating public lobby displays for city council meetings—when public officials see progress, they are happy, which often converts into positive feedback to project leaders

These activities can keep you and your communities' interest intact over the long run. Staying motivated ensures that you will recognize and be ready to accept opportunity when it comes your way. Inevitably, such efforts will allow you to enjoy the great work you are doing in your community.

projects (i.e., **what**) of varying complexities and in several locations that, when completed in their totality, are envisioned to contribute to a stronger sense of community and pride (i.e., **why**). (In a real project action plan, this section as well as those that follow would be written in greater detail.)

- **Team Members Critical to Implementation:** This section describes **who** will serve as team members and leaders throughout your implementation efforts, acknowledging their valued role in attaining your placemaking vision. (Note: This is a very important section because, after all, individuals, organizations, and businesses are the most important resource for realizing placemaking projects.)

The envisioned POAB projects are important to different neighborhood residents and community groups (i.e., **who**). Each project entails the involvement of varying public agencies and private businesses that are integral to the project approval process or have access to skills and resources needed to implement (i.e., **who**).

- **Key Action Steps, Schedule, and Budget:** This section answers **how** and **when** the placemaking project will come to life by outlining and describing key steps (or actions), and the corresponding timeframes, needed to occur to achieve the complete placemaking projects. This section describes how funding, in-kind services, volunteerism, promotion, donations, grant writing, approvals, and other details of the project will occur. **How much** is also discussed in this section, in terms of estimated or probable costs (as applicable) for each project.

For each POAB project identified in the vision section, specific steps would be described that summarize how implementation would occur (including probable costs) as well as associated timeframes (i.e., when).

- **Implementation Matrix:** This section of the action plan is intended to provide users with an at-a-glance summary of "what, where, why, when, who, how much, and how" for the POAB project or vision plan.

Figure 4-5. Implementation matrices provide a framework for organizing more complex POAB projects.

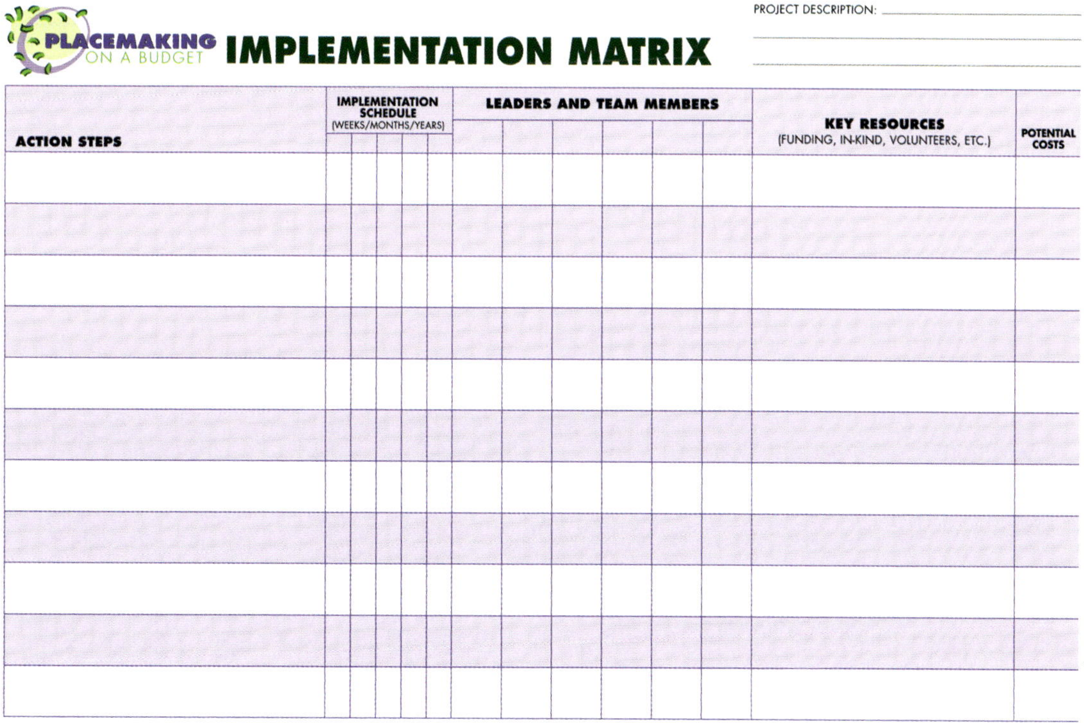

PLACEMAKING ON A BUDGET — IMPLEMENTATION MATRIX

PROJECT DESCRIPTION: _____

ACTION STEPS	IMPLEMENTATION SCHEDULE (WEEKS/MONTHS/YEARS)	LEADERS AND TEAM MEMBERS	KEY RESOURCES (FUNDING, IN-KIND, VOLUNTEERS, ETC.)	POTENTIAL COSTS

Through the use of an implementation matrix (see Figure 4-5), an organized approach can be outlined to help communities more effectively and efficiently achieve their envisioned projects.

Determining which organizational tool to use for implementing POAB projects requires a number of considerations, among them the audience (e.g., who will be the key implementers, what implementation experience do they have), the scale and complexity of project, and the timeframe (e.g., will the project require a multi-phased approach). Most important to POAB projects is to fully consider the multiple aspects of implementation for each undertaking to optimize efficiencies and effectiveness.

CONCLUSION

POAB projects happen through the simultaneous alignment of champions, community energy, resources, and actions. Consistent and continuous storytelling pertaining to each envisioned project—its roots in community values and its value to the community—help reinforce the potential for implementation. The more organized POAB projects are, and the more familiar their stories are, the more efficiently they tend to be implemented and maintained as an enduring community asset.

Appendix A. Toolkits

CHAPTER 2 TOOLKIT

The following POAB worksheets (see the CD-ROM for the forms to print them out or xerox them from the appendices) are useful for identifying community values, canvases, and projects.

- *POAB Worksheet #1: Our Community Values*. (Figure A-1) This worksheet provides a focused area for brainstorming those values pertaining to your community's history and culture, natural environment, and other community attributes.

- *POAB Worksheet #2: Canvases in Our Community*. (Figure A-2) This worksheet provides a focused area for brainstorming those architectural, landscape, and infrastructure canvases in your community that offer opportunities for a POAB project to occur.

- *POAB Worksheet #3: Community Values/Community Canvases.* (Figure A-3) This worksheet provides a tool for matching up community values (identified with POAB Worksheet #1) with canvases (identified with POAB Worksheet #2) as a means of inspiring POAB project ideas (see POAB Worksheet #4).

- *POAB Worksheet #4: Projects*. (Figure A-4) This worksheet is useful for documenting POAB project ideas that come to mind when comparing community values and community canvases (identified with POAB Worksheet #3).

As with all of POAB worksheets, please duplicate and use them as necessary to help identify POAB projects in your community.

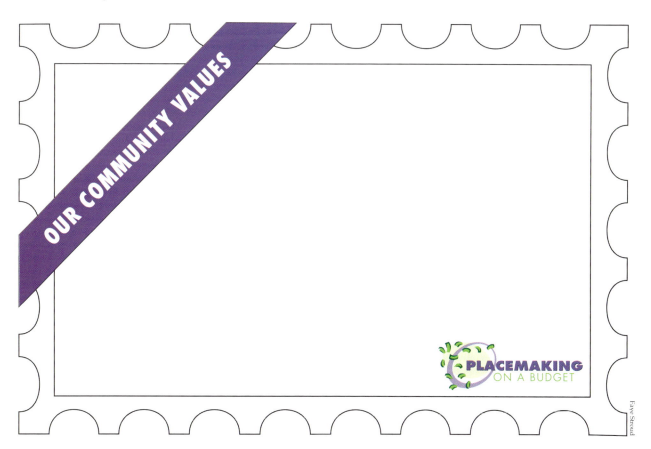

Figure A-1. POAB Worksheet #1: Our Community Values.

Figure A-2. POAB Worksheet #2: *Canvases in Our Community.*

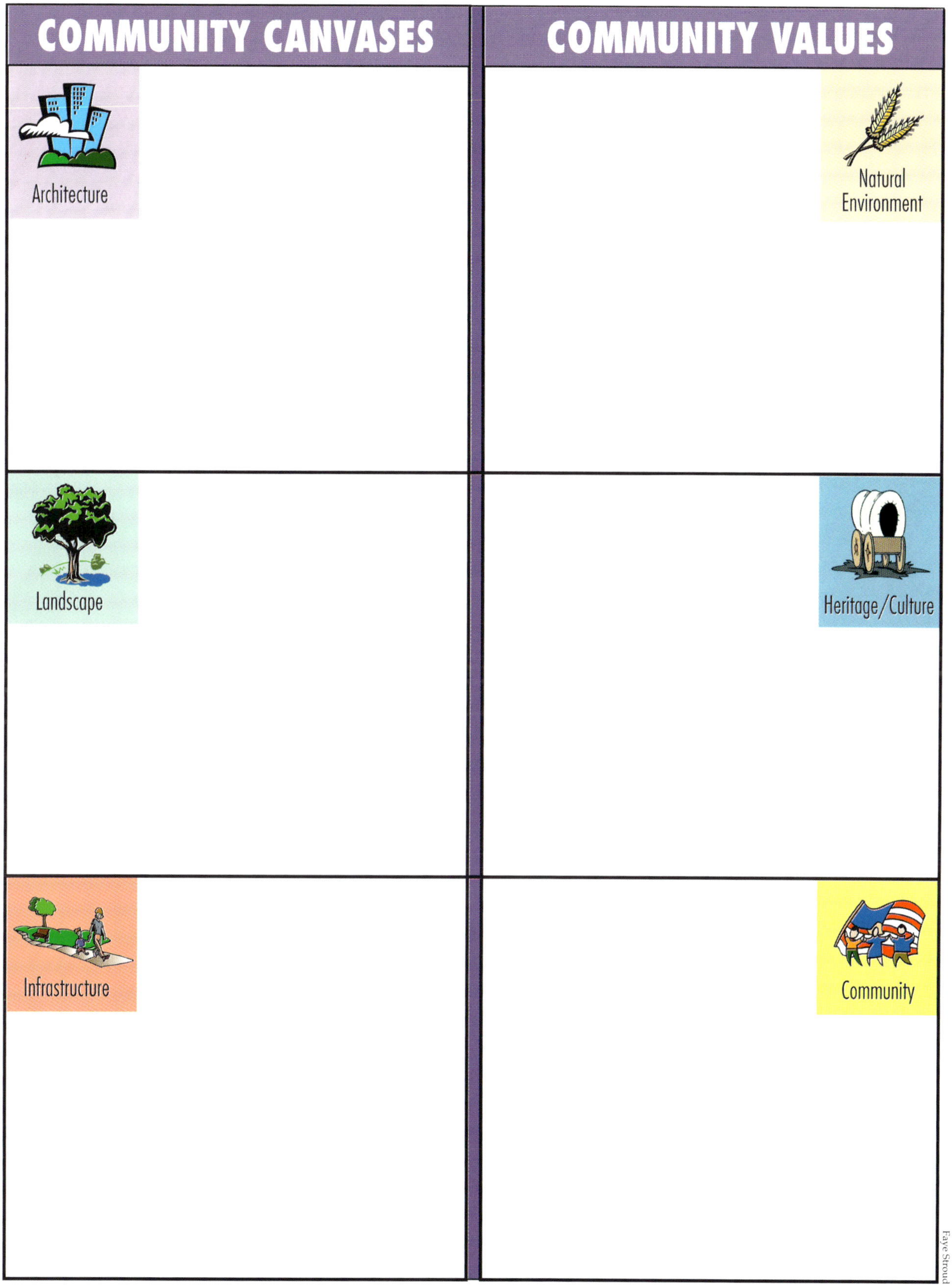

Figure A-3. POAB Worksheet #3: *Community Canvases/Community Values.*

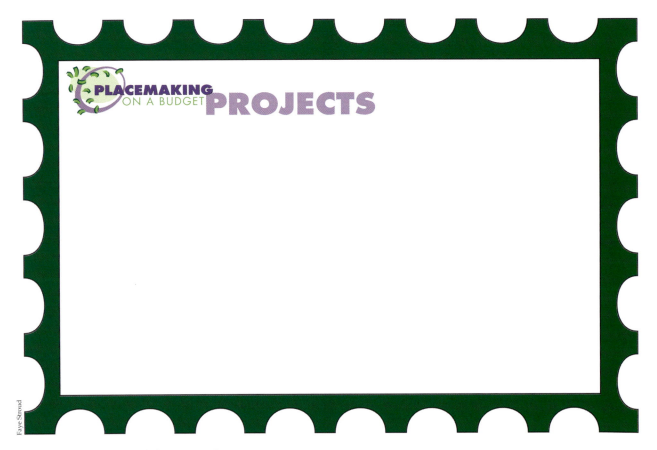

Figure A-4. POAB Worksheet #4: Projects.

CHAPTER 3 TOOLKIT

POAB worksheet #5 is useful for brainstorming potential POAB resources in your community.

- *POAB Worksheet #5: Resource Puzzle.* (Figure A-5) This puzzle worksheet identifies a number of different groups that may be able to serve as resources for your projects. Use this tool to brainstorm specific business names, individuals, groups, and organizations for your POAB projects.

As with all of the POAB worksheets, please duplicate and use as necessary to help discover possible resources for your projects.

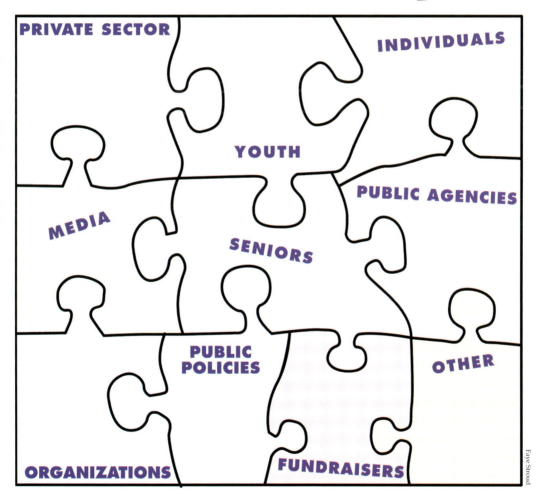

Figure A-5. There are a myriad of different resources available to implement POAB projects.

CHAPTER 4 TOOLKIT

POAB worksheets 6, 7, 8, and 9 are useful for organizing your POAB project ideas and the implementation components necessary to realize your projects.

- *POAB Worksheet #6: Project Worksheet.* (Figure A-6) This worksheet provides a brainstorming tool to implement simple POAB projects. It is intended to help answer each of the seven implementation questions: what, where, why, when, who, how, and how much.

- *POAB Worksheet #7: Implementation Matrix.* (Figure A-7) This worksheet provides an organized approach for documenting who, what, when, where, why, how and how much for your POAB projects. It is intended to serve as a tool that is regularly referenced and updated.

- *POAB Worksheet #8: Project Details.* (Figure A-8) This worksheet provides a formal-looking graphic tool for describing and illustrating your POAB project (as identified using the worksheets for Chapter 2, which are above). This worksheet can be used to help communicate and market your POAB project and should be used in conjunction with POAB Worksheet #8, which focuses on project resources and implementation steps.

- *POAB Worksheet #9: Project Resources/Project Implementation Steps.* (Figure A-9) This worksheet provides a formal-looking graphic to be used in tandem with POAB Worksheet #7 for laying out project resources and implementation steps. The contents of this worksheet may be compiled from the information generated using the worksheets identified in Chapter 3 (i.e., resources), as well as this chapter (i.e., implementation steps).

As with all of POAB worksheets, please duplicate and use them as necessary to help identify POAB projects in your community. You will find copies on the CD-ROM accompanying this PAS Report.

Project Worksheet

WHAT? _____

WHERE? _____

WHY? _____

WHEN? _____

WHO? _____

HOW MUCH? _____

HOW? _____

Figure A-6. POAB Worksheet.

Figure A-7. POAB Worksheet #7: Implementation Matrix.

(Above) **Figure A-8.** *POAB Worksheet #8: Project Details; (below)* **Figure A-9.** *POAB Worksheet #9: Project Resources/Project Implementation Steps.*

Appendix B. List of References

Bird, S. E. 2002. "It Makes Sense to Us: Cultural Identity in Local Legends of Place." *Journal of Contemporary Ethnography* 31, no. 5: 519–48.

Brown, B. B., and D.D. Perkins. 1992. "Disruption in Place Attachment." In *Place Attachment*, edited by I. Altman and S.M. Low, 279-304. New York: Plenum.

Cohen, A. P. 1985. *The Symbolic Construction of Community.* Chichester, England: Ellis Horwood.

Cresswell, T. 1996. *In Place, Out of Place: Geography, Ideology and Transgression.* Minneapolis: University of Minnesota Press.

Dane, S. G. 1997. *Main Street Success Stories.* Washington, D.C.: National Main Street Center.

Entrikin, J. N. 1996. "Place and Region 2." *Progress in Human Geography* 20, no. 2: 215–21.

Greider, T., and L. Garkovich. 1994. "Landscapes: The Social Construction of Nature and the Environment." *Rural Sociology* 59, no. 1: 1–24.

Jackson, J. B. 1994. *A Sense of Place, A Sense of Time.* New Haven, Conn.: Yale University Press.

Jacobi, M., and D. Stokols. 1983. "The Role of Tradition in Group-Environment Relations." In *Environmental Psychology: Directions and Perspectives*, edited by N. R. Feimer and E. S. Geller, 151–79. New York: Praeger.

Johnstone, B. 1990. *Stories, Community, and Place: Narratives from Middle America.* Bloomington: Indiana University Press.

Kemmis, D. 1990. *Community and the Politics of Place.* Norman: University of Oklahoma Press.

Kretzmann, J. P., and J. L. McKnight. 1993. *Building Communities from the Inside Out: A Path Toward Finding and Mobilizing a Community's Assets.* Evanston, Ill.: Institute for Policy Research.

Kunstler, J. H. 1993. *The Geography of Nowhere.* New York: Touchstone.

Lepofsky, J., and J.C. Fraser. 2003. "Building Community Citizens: Claiming the Right to Place-Making in the City." *Urban Studies* 40, no. 1: 127–43.

Reed, J., V.R. Payton, and S. Bond. 1998. "The Importance of Place for Older People Moving into Care Homes." *Social Science & Medicine* 46, no. 7: 859–68.

Relph, E. 1976. *Place and Placelessness.* London: Pion Limited.

Robertson, K. A. 1999. "Can Small-City Downtowns Remain Viable? A National Study of Development Issues and Strategies." *Journal of the American Planning Association* 65, no. 3: 270–83.

Ryden, K. C. 1993. *Mapping the Invisible Landscape: Folklore, Writing, and the Sense of Place.* Iowa City: University of Iowa Press.

Schneekloth, L. H., and R. G. Shibley. 1995. *Placemaking: The Art and Practice of Building Communities.* New York: John Wiley and Sons.

Stedman, R. C. 2002. "Towards a Social Psychology of Place: Predicting Behavior from Place-Based Cognitions, Attitudes, and Identity." *Environment and Behavior* 34, no. 5: 561–82.

Stegner, W. E. 1992. *Where the Bluebird Sings to the Lemonade Springs: Living and Writing in the West.* New York: Random House.

Stokowski, P. A. 2002. "Languages of Place and Discourses of Power: Constructing New Senses of Place." *Journal of Leisure Research* 34, no. 4: 368–83.

Vandergeest, P., and E. M. DuPuis, eds. *Creating the Countryside: The Politics of Rural and Environmental Discourse.* Philadelphia, Penn.: Temple University Press.

RECENT PLANNING ADVISORY SERVICE REPORTS

Making Great Communities Happen

The American Planning Association provides leadership in the development of vital communities by advocating excellence in community planning, promoting education and citizen empowerment, and providing the tools and support necessary to effect positive change.

482. Planning and Zoning for Concentrated Animal Feeding Operations. Jim Schwab. December 1998. 44pp.

483/484. Planning for Post-Disaster Recovery and Reconstruction. Jim Schwab, et al. December 1998. 346pp.

485. Traffic Sheds, Rural Highway Capacity, and Growth Management. Lane Kendig with Stephen Tocknell. March 1999. 24pp.

486. Youth Participation in Community Planning. Ramona Mullahey, Yve Susskind, and Barry Checkoway. June 1999. 70pp.

489/490. Aesthetics, Community Character, and the Law. Christopher J. Duerksen and R. Matthew Goebel. December 1999. 154pp.

493. Transportation Impact Fees and Excise Taxes: A Survey of 16 Jurisdictions. Connie Cooper. July 2000. 62pp.

494. Incentive Zoning: Meeting Urban Design and Affordable Housing Objectives. Marya Morris. September 2000. 64pp.

495/496. Everything You Always Wanted To Know About Regulating Sex Businesses. Eric Damian Kelly and Connie Cooper. December 2000. 168pp.

497/498. Parks, Recreation, and Open Spaces: An Agenda for the 21st Century. Alexander Garvin. December 2000. 72pp.

499. Regulating Home-Based Businesses in the Twenty-First Century. Charles Wunder. December 2000. 37pp.

500/501. Lights, Camera, Community Video. Cabot Orton, Keith Spiegel, and Eddie Gale. April 2001. 76pp.

502. Parks and Economic Development. John L. Crompton. November 2001. 74pp.

503/504. Saving Face: How Corporate Franchise Design Can Respect Community Identity (revised edition). Ronald Lee Fleming. February 2002. 118pp.

505. Telecom Hotels: A Planners Guide. Jennifer Evans-Crowley. March 2002. 31pp.

506/507. Old Cities/Green Cities: Communities Transform Unmanaged Land. J. Blaine Bonham, Jr., Gerri Spilka, and Darl Rastorfer. March 2002. 123pp.

508. Performance Guarantees for Government Permit Granting Authorities. Wayne Feiden and Raymond Burby. July 2002. 80pp.

509. Street Vending: A Survey of Ideas and Lessons for Planners. Jennifer Ball. August 2002. 44pp.

510/511. Parking Standards. Edited by Michael Davidson and Fay Dolnick. November 2002. 181pp.

512. Smart Growth Audits. Jerry Weitz and Leora Susan Waldner. November 2002. 56pp.

513/514. Regional Approaches to Affordable Housing. Stuart Meck, Rebecca Retzlaff, and James Schwab. February 2003. 271pp.

515. Planning for Street Connectivity: Getting from Here to There. Susan Handy, Robert G. Paterson, and Kent Butler. May 2003. 95pp.

516. Jobs-Housing Balance. Jerry Weitz. November 2003. 41pp.

517. Community Indicators. Rhonda Phillips. December 2003. 46pp.

518/519. Ecological Riverfront Design. Betsy Otto, Kathleen McCormick, and Michael Leccese. March 2004. 177pp.

520. Urban Containment in the United States. Arthur C. Nelson and Casey J. Dawkins. March 2004. 130pp.

521/522. A Planners Dictionary. Edited by Michael Davidson and Fay Dolnick. April 2004. 460pp.

523/524. Crossroads, Hamlet, Village, Town (revised edition). Randall Arendt. April 2004. 142pp.

525. E-Government. Jennifer Evans–Cowley and Maria Manta Conroy. May 2004. 41pp.

526. Codifying New Urbanism. Congress for the New Urbanism. May 2004. 97pp.

527. Street Graphics and the Law. Daniel Mandelker with Andrew Bertucci and William Ewald. August 2004. 133pp.

528. Too Big, Boring, or Ugly: Planning and Design Tools to Combat Monotony, the Too-big House, and Teardowns. Lane Kendig. December 2004. 103pp.

529/530. Planning for Wildfires. James Schwab and Stuart Meck. February 2005. 126pp.

531. Planning for the Unexpected: Land-Use Development and Risk. Laurie Johnson, Laura Dwelley Samant, and Suzanne Frew. February 2005. 59pp.

532. Parking Cash Out. Donald C. Shoup. March 2005. 119pp.

533/534. Landslide Hazards and Planning. James C. Schwab, Paula L. Gori, and Sanjay Jeer, Project Editors. September 2005. 209pp.

535. The Four Supreme Court Land-Use Decisions of 2005: Separating Fact from Fiction. August 2005. 193pp.

536. Placemaking on a Budget: Improving Small Towns, Neighborhoods, and Downtowns Without Spending a Lot of Money. December 2005. 133pp.

For price information, please go to www.planning.org or call 312-431-9100 and ask for the Planners Book Service. The web site also contains a complete subject and chronological index to the PAS Report series.